My Mother Never Taught Me Songs

~Memoirs of growing up in an imperfect world~

Lilian S. Barber

TRAFFORD
USA · Canada · UK · Ireland

© Copyright 2006 Lilian S. Barber.
All rights reserved. No part of this publication may be reproduced, stored in a retrieval system, or transmitted, in any form or by any means, electronic, mechanical, photocopying, recording, or otherwise, without the written prior permission of the author.

Note for Librarians: A cataloguing record for this book is available from Library and Archives Canada at www.collectionscanada.ca/amicus/index-e.html
ISBN 1-4120-9997-8

Printed in Victoria, BC, Canada. Printed on paper with minimum 30% recycled fibre.
Trafford's print shop runs on "green energy" from solar, wind and other environmentally-friendly power sources.

Offices in Canada, USA, Ireland and UK

Book sales for North America and international:
Trafford Publishing, 6E–2333 Government St.,
Victoria, BC V8T 4P4 CANADA
phone 250 383 6864 (toll-free 1 888 232 4444)
fax 250 383 6804; email to orders@trafford.com

Book sales in Europe:
Trafford Publishing (UK) Limited, 9 Park End Street, 2nd Floor
Oxford, UK OX1 1HH UNITED KINGDOM
phone +44 (0)1865 722 113 (local rate 0845 230 9601)
facsimile +44 (0)1865 722 868; info.uk@trafford.com

Order online at:
trafford.com/06-1753

10 9 8 7 6 5 4 3 2 1

INTRODUCTION

As far back as I can remember people have been telling me that I should write a book. However, for the longest time no one ever really had any idea what kind of book I should write—at least not a very good idea. In that respect, the suggestion that I write a book is something like the very resolute idea my mother continued to express while I was in the terminal stages of high school that I should find a job in a "nice office". It didn't matter what kind of office this might be or what connection that office would have with any form of productivity. To her, as to many women of her period and ilk, there was no apparent palpable correlation between an office and whatever business of which it might be a part and for which it performed its paper chase. An office appeared to stand alone, an entity by itself that existed to supply employment for a number of girls and women. For my mother there were only four choices of workplace for a woman—an office, a store, a factory or a restaurant. "Nice" girls from good families worked in an office. As a workplace, a store, of whatever type, was a step down from an office, and truly lower class girls found work in factories or eating places. It was as simple as that. It used to really distress me that I could not make my mother understand that an office, per se, could simply not exist as an independent unit. In fact, what I came to call the "nice office syndrome" used to plague me so much that it once was part of an inspiration for a short story, one that is more like a fictional essay, if indeed there should be such a creature in existence among the various forms of writing.

Anyway, to go back a little in time, shortly before my fiftieth birthday I decided that I really did want to put some of my abundance of short features, sketches, essays, poems and impressions into book form and attempt to do something about having such a volume published. Some of my work had appeared in various magazines, house organs and newspapers. I had even been paid for some of these writings; but I had never quite managed to write the all too elusive Great American Novel. I was quite aware then as I am now that I never would, and that my writing forte lies in nonfiction bits and pieces; and what does one do with THOSE? Is there any kind of market for fragments of the memoirs of someone not quite memorable enough to write an autobiography? All are impressions of people, events and circumstances that have been shaped over nearly three quarters of a century of living on a beautiful, interesting and sometimes even awe inspiring but decidedly less than perfect planet.

The projected appearance of "Ruptured Rainbow" by my fiftieth birthday was interrupted by months of work on another book, a very definite one that, believe it or not, I was asked to write. It was a special interest book about Italian Greyhounds, a charismatic breed of dog with which my husband and I have been deeply involved since 1966. This kind of writing leaves no leeway for the type of personal expression I had intended to be the hallmark of "Rainbow," but for the time being my original project was grounded.

The first Italian Greyhound book was followed by another, more expanded breed volume called "The Complete Italian Greyhound"; so "Ruptured Rainbow" once again was put on hold. For a year or two after the publication of "The Complete Italian Greyhound" I felt that my need to write a book and have it published had been fulfilled. Then, slowly but insidiously, "Rainbow" started to creep back into my consciousness and work on it began again. However, in 1992 my publisher, Joan Cooper of Italian Greyhound Productions, asked me if I would revise, update and expand "The Complete Italian Greyhound". Once again the Rainbow project was shelved.

In May of 1994 one of my Italian Greyhound fancier friends, Judy Murff, called me from Wyoming and asked me what I was going to do for an encore now that my work on the new IG book was completed. I told her about "Ruptured Rainbow," and she was intrigued. She asked me to send her a sample of what it would include, and I forwarded to her a printout of the report card chapter, which now forms the preface to this book. Almost immediately there was another phone call from Judy. She thought I should write more about my experiences before, during and after World War II and how the Holocaust had affected my life. What fascinated Judy the most was that my story could be written from the viewpoint of the young child who had lived it.

I had, indeed, thought about that myself more than once, but I had always mentally scrapped the idea. After all, I did not see with my own eyes the horror so many others had seen. I had not actually lived through it nor had I seen the slaughter and misery first hand. Although much of the time I had kept a diary, I was not another Anne Frank. I was very much alive, and I did not as much as have a tattooed number on my forearm.

Nothing physically really bad had ever happened to me. There were hundreds of thousands like me who had escaped with their skins intact to make a new life in another country. What stories could I possibly tell that would be of interest to readers?

Judy said she could hardly wait to read more and insisted that I work on a book about my experiences.

Why write a book? Why write anything at all? What does it take to be a writer in the first place? I think the first two questions can be answered by explaining that the urge to write is simply a need to communicate. Perhaps, as in my case, one has grown up without anyone to listen when a good listener was very much needed. Children of all ages are desperate to be heard, and if there is no one there to lend an ear, the result can be disastrous or, as in my case, it can be funneled into a passion for writing. The written word travels further and more easily than a message spoken, and if the first person to encounter it has no interest in it—it can go along down the line to someone who does care.

When I was a pre-teen and then a teenager my parents were very much taken up with their own problems, which were, of course, far greater and more significant than mine. They did the best they could, but neither of them had been well equipped to cope with what life had tossed at them. The monumental change in circumstances and lifestyle when they were forced to flee Germany just ahead of the Holocaust had left them with little time or energy to deal with the plight, real and imagined, of a lonely child. My peers during those World War II years were far less sophisticated than today's youngsters and were loath to accept someone who appeared to be quite different from themselves. I struggled to overcome those differences, but I could not lose my accent quickly enough nor could we afford to replace my foreign clothing with the current local styles. Most of all, I tried much too hard to be liked and to make friends—an effort that often serves only to drive away the desired result. Consequently, failing to connect, I retreated to the library and found my best companions in books. They taught me, among a myriad other things, how to use my new language as a tool for expression. Books, too, served as the travel agency that lent wings to my mind.

Knowledge of the language, its words and grammar, is like a set of tools. Anyone with the means can buy tools—even good tools. Basic English, just as good tools can be bought, can be learned. The added ingredient, similar to mechanical aptitude for the person with implements for work, is an impressionable intellect, the power to observe, to interpret, to associate, to understand and to remember. To write effectively it helps also to have the capacity, in the broadest sense, for love and for hate and to accept the fact that often there is a very fragile line of demarcation between the two. Like most of us less than perfect humans, I have loved people and things both tangible and not that I had no business loving and have time and again found myself hating what should have been understood and loved. However, a person who has dealt with those types of feelings usually finds it much more possible to communicate incisively than one who observes the world with bland non-involvement.

In these pages there is some pathos and some humor, a little bitterness, some joy and the viable remnants of a sense of wonder. There is a little of nature and some reverence as well for the miscellaneous works and efforts, successful and failed, of man. There may be an occasional shock, just as there is in life itself; and, for those who think they know me well, perhaps a surprise or two. There is obscenity where something appeared, to me, to be obscene. I find the power of the four letter word a painfully inadequate armory against frustration, but sometimes, it being the only available weapon short of physical violence, I consider it better to commit outrage upon someone's ears or eyes than to turn anger completely inward to fester with the risk of an eventual major and traumatic explosion.

I have found that writing—articles, letters, poems, anything at all expressive—is an exquisite means of venting frustrations in a creative way or at least non-destructively. It is quite possible in the depths of anger to write meaningfully. Consequently, I prefer to be angry to being sad, since sadness and depression tend to paralyze whereas anger galvanizes.

My mother used to sing, but for lack of time or energy or understanding—or most likely a combination of all three—she never taught me songs. That may be the main reason for my having written this book.

Lilian S. Barber, June, 2006

PREFACE

REPORT CARD

It happened in the late months of 1938.

At that time all of the 40,000 inhabitants of Rottenburg am Neckar knew one another. At least they all knew that there were only four Jewish families in the little German farm town. There were two families of Horkheimers, the Bauers and another family, the name of which has slipped my mind. I was seven and a half years old, and I had started school almost a year earlier. I liked attending school, although the aging, grizzled schoolmaster was very strict. I had seen him hit several of the girls simply because they were unprepared with the answer to a question, and I don't think that there was a boy in the class who had not had the seat of his trousers warmed by the master's stick for some infringement like neglecting to bring a handkerchief to school. Nevertheless, I liked school. I liked to read, to write on the little slates on which German students did their lessons, and to make the bookmarks and doilies that we assembled during our Saturday crafts classes. Besides, school was about the only place left where I could still play with other children of my age. For some reason unknown to me at the time, my friends had stopped coming to my house to play. Not even the big sandbox I had in my yard and which had once been the envy of every child in Rottenburg could attract playmates any longer. I did not learn until some time later that the little girls who had been my best friends had been given dolls and other toys in exchange for their promise not to play with me anymore. It was later still before I completely understood that the only reason for this machination was that I was Jewish.

It was a beautiful, sunny day. The sky was a cloudless blue, and the tall grain that grew by the side of the dirt road not far from our house shone a brilliant yellow and rippled gently in a refreshing breeze. I was as happy as a seven year old could be. I had just received my report card, my very first report card; and it was a good one. Oh, it had not been the best in the class; it was merely a very good card, but I felt very proud of what I had accomplished. I held it gaily aloft as I went skipping across town toward home. One of our neighbors, Mrs. Metzger, I believe, smiled at me as I came by. She was one of the few who had not as yet turned a cold shoulder toward us. I think I was so happy that not even Aunt Jenny's grumpy, barking German shepherd dog frightened me as he usually did when I passed him. I had always had a deathly fear of that dog, but as I swung through the gate, I scarcely noticed him.

We had a fairly large garden. At one end was my Aunt Jenny's house, and at the other end was the white, two story stone house that my parents and grandparents had jointly bought three years earlier. My grandparents lived on the upper floor; and my mother and father and I lived downstairs. Aunt Jenny and her husband were actually my great aunt and uncle.

I passed the circular rock garden that my mother had worked so hard to cultivate and ran by the bare apple trees, their leaves long gone for the year. Under the outspread branches of the gigantic, ancient pear tree that served as a picnic tent on warm summer days and around to the doorway I went. Our door was always open, since someone was always at home.

"Mother!" I screamed, in German, of course. "Guess what?"

There was no answer. I continued on my bounding way into the living room. The first person I saw was an elderly woman who had been a close friend of ours. I hadn't expected her to be there. I looked around a little disappointedly, still waving my now nearly forgotten report card. Then I saw my mother. She was sitting on the sofa, her face turned downward; but I could see that she had been crying.

Our friend tried to lead me out of the room, but my exuberance had returned; and I persistently waved my report card under my mother's nose. I think I remember tears beginning to form in her red-rimmed eyes, but she also made a brave attempt to catch my enthusiasm. She skimmed over the card, but she just couldn't seem to find anything good to say to me.

It was only then that I realized that something must be terribly the matter. My mother had always been a spirited, high-strung, demonstrative woman, and now all she was doing was to sit and stare blankly at my prized report card as if she had no comprehension whatsoever of what she was seeing.

My grandparents had gone to Mannheim to visit some relatives, and my mother had been alone in the house when it had happened. It was not until that evening that I found out and was able to understand, if only partially, what had taken place. Early that morning some police officials had come to the house and had taken my father with them. Later one of them had returned with my father's watch, ring and pocket money. He had offered no explanation.

The next day we learned that my father had been taken to the concentration camp at Dachau. Why? 40,000 people knew that the Bauers were one of the four families in Rottenburg who were Jews. In the Germany of 1938 no other reason was necessary.

Gertrude, Siegfried and Lilian Bauer in 1938. These photos were taken for our passports when we left Germany.

CHAPTER ONE

1938

My cousin Ingrid is four years younger than I. She was a beautiful, towheaded child with the blue eyes and fair skin of her Aryan mother. She was the first child to be born into any segment of my immediate family who was not completely Jewish. I was too young to understand much about the circumstances of her parents' marriage and how the remainder of the family felt about it, but even at a very early age I knew that Ingrid was different; and I was extremely jealous of her. It seems that there were always comparisons made, and Ingrid was pointed out to be the most beautiful child ever to grace the Horkheimer clan. She was also graceful and endearing.

My uncle Rudolf, Ingrid's father, was my mother's younger brother. Rudolf was quite handsome, and he was brilliant to the point of genius. He excelled as an engineer, as a photographer and as an imaginative inventor. He also was musically talented and played well enough that he could have been a professional concert violinist. From what I have been able to piece together, he was also quite good at being a con artist.

Rudolf saw and understood the gathering storm in Germany early and, before anything bad had actually begun to happen, moved with his wife and daughter to Bolivia. On their way there they stopped in Rottenburg for a brief visit and to say good-bye. His attempts to persuade the Horkheimers, my mother's parents, to make plans for an exodus of their own fell on deaf ears. Albert and Rosa Horkheimer only half believed that the Nazi juggernaut was making plans to wipe out all the Jews in Germany. They really did not want to believe it, and they felt that they were too old to weather the drastic changes that emigration to another country would engender. My father was ambivalent and undecided about the need to leave Germany, and, of course, my mother verbalized no views of her own. She would go along with whatever my father considered to be right.

Rudolf and his family lived in Berlin and came once or twice a year to visit us. On each of these occasions there was a great deal of fuss made over Ingrid for reasons that I failed to understand, and they were never explained to me. I did understand, however, when my mother chided me for being clumsy when Ingrid was so graceful and for being so slow about so many things compared to how quickly and well Ingrid did them in spite of her being nearly four years my junior.

One specific comparison, other than Ingrid's athletic ability and my lack of it, that still rankles in my mind involved the eating of apples. Apples were a very important food in Germany during the thirties. Lacking the huge variety of fruits we see in the United States, German people ate apples in many different forms. Besides apple strudel, apple pie and other stewed or baked apple desserts apples were frequently eaten raw, either peeled and sliced or as they came from the tree.

My mother was right about my being pokey and slow about many things, one of which was eating—especially eating foods I did not particularly like. Raw apples constituted one of those foods. It could take me half an hour to unenthusiastically gnaw my way through a medium sized apple.

At some time during Ingrid's final visit to our house my mother, who was a very handsome woman given to quick, nervous movements, tired of seeing my lackluster performance with an apple. She grasped me by the arm and led me to where my little cousin was enjoying her fruit.

"Look at that," she said, pointing to Ingrid. "See how much better she eats an apple than you do. Look what good, big bites she takes!"

I was embarrassed and annoyed, but I knew better than to talk back to my mother. Talking back, even politely, in those days was considered a cardinal sin and would result in an immediate slap across the mouth.

    She went on. "You take such little baby bites, and your cousin eats her apple like a grownup. Listen to her— *rrrhab, rrrhab, rrrhab, rrrhab!*"

    My mother's portrayal of that sound is something I will never forget. I don't think the incident served to speed up my eating of apples, which did not happen until many years later; but it has contributed to my having the same reaction when I hear someone bite into an apple that most people feel when a fingernail grates across a blackboard.

⋘⋙

Whenever my uncle Rudolf came to visit, he and my mother would play endless classical duets—he on the violin and she on the piano. At such times my mother forced me to sit quietly and listen to them, seemingly for hours, with the hope that I would gain an appreciation for classical music. Oddly enough, I did learn to love it in spite of my early unwillingness to sit still—and to regret that a minor grievance for which the Holocaust is also to blame is that I never received the kind of formal musical education other Horkheimer children had always received.

    My mother's main musical training had been in voice, and she had at one time aspired to become an opera singer. The piano was added so that she would be able to accompany herself when she practiced her singing. Indeed she had a wonderful singing voice and would definitely have had potential for a career on the operatic stage. Later, when I became a rabid opera fan, my mother led me to believe that my father had asked her when they married to give up her desire to become a professional singer. I went through my teen years and much of my adulthood blaming my father for the sad fact that I did not have a mother who was a famous opera star. It was only after my mother's death in 1991 that some distant relatives pointed out to me that my father had made no actual objection to my mother pursuing an operatic career but that it was much easier for her to blame him than to admit that the endless hard work and extensive demands of preparing to become a professional singer in grand opera were more than she was willing to tackle.

It was only a few months after Rudolf and his family left for South America that the trouble really started. At first my family remained secure in the belief that the small, close-knit little town of Rottenburg would be a safe haven. There was, of course, no television in those days to inform and incite the public. Radio news made far less of an impact, and much of it was edited by the Nazi government before it was allowed to go out over the air and reach the general public.

The election came and went, an election in which a "no" vote against Adolf Hitler, the only candidate, brought swift and severe retribution, some of which in the form of what was called "Krystallnacht", or "Night of Broken Glass". We learned that very graphically on the night the Archbishop's residence was raided, the windows broken, the furniture and artifacts destroyed. The Archbishop escaped—only temporarily, I believe. He had voted against Hitler, making him immediately an enemy of the state.

The violence against the Archbishop was only a small segment of Krystallnacht. Broken windows, destroyed property and beatings occurred en masse all over Germany that night, not only against the Jews and political dissidents but against gypsies, homosexuals, people with birth defects or mental disorders and any others the Nazi regime found to be against their image of perfection in a master race.

It was not long after this that my father was taken to Dachau.

That was a very unhappy and stressful time for my entire family, although my memories of it are more in an over-all impression than in any detail. I suppose everyone felt that I was too young to understand what was happening, and I was not told very much. The adults—my mother and my grandparents and sometimes my great aunt and uncle—talked in whispers whenever they thought I might overhear. I did not understand what they were saying, but even at seven years of age I understood that those were very frightened whispers, and the words were words of fear and trepidation. In spite of not understanding, I felt terrified a good part of the time.

For us, all normal activities except those essential to our survival ceased. There was no longer any joy or laughter in the household, nor were there any outings or games. The only place I was allowed to go was to school, and shortly that, too, ended when the Nazi government decreed that Jewish children were no longer allowed to attend public school. The time seemed like an eternity to a frightened and solitary little girl, although my father's imprisonment actually lasted only a little over two months.

There were no Jewish schools in Rottenburg for me to attend, and my grandfather tried very hard to fill in and to make up for the lack of formal schooling available to me. We had daily reading, writing and arithmetic lessons in his study, a large, well lit room where he read and sometimes worked in pastels. There were good paintings—all originals—on the walls and a collection of antiques. There were also many leather bound books. He sat me down at his desk as we worked. He sat next to me in a leather armchair. Although he was probably no more than sixty, he always looked so very old to me, with his bald head and little square, gray mustache. It was the same style mustache as Hitler's. I suppose it was the fashion at the time even for Jewish men.

I had been to public school just long enough to begin to write in German script. I was a good student and learned quickly, but no one seemed to care. It was difficult for a seven year old to understand adult priorities. Eventually, there were multitudes of other things for grandfather Albert to do, and the daily teaching sessions came to an end. I truly missed them. I had enjoyed learning while it had been available to me, and there was nothing much to replace it.

The factory that my father and grandfather owned together had to be run. My father, until his arrest, had been doing most of it but now my grandfather had to take over. He began to leave the house early in the morning and, like my father had been doing, returned for lunch and a little rest and then went back to the factory in mid afternoon. He would come home between seven and eight in the evening for supper. That was the typical work day in Germany. He also had almost daily meetings with the town's chief of police and other officials. Sometimes these took place in our house, but I was never allowed to be present or to overhear the goings-on.

I learned later that the meetings involved payments in varying but large amounts to several different high up people in an effort to obtain my father's release from the concentration camp.

Eventually the bribes paid off, and one day my father came home. They had told him as he left Dachau that he had a certain length of time—I believe it was two or three months—to take his family and leave the country or he would be sent back to be imprisoned—permanently, and so would the rest of the Bauer and Horkheimer families.

He spoke little of his experiences in Dachau, especially not in front of me. However, he had lost a great deal of weight, and his normally healthy complexion had turned sallow. Among what little I was able to catch from his chronicles was that the prisoners were nearly starved to death and were often forced to do rigid calisthenics for long periods of time. Those who stumbled or were unable to do the exercises to the satisfaction of the guards were severely beaten with nightsticks and whips.

Much of what followed is quite vague in my mind. As had been the custom, no one told me anything nor allowed me to hear much about what was going on. There were nonstop family discussions, some of which became rather heated. I think those involved the very set decision of my grandparents not to leave Germany and the pleas and entreaties of my parents to attempt to change their minds. My father, who had seen for himself what was happening to the Jews of Germany, was determined to convince them to go with us, wherever we might wind up having to go.

Many letters were sent to the United States. It was necessary to get a relative in America to guarantee that we would not become a public liability. We had absolutely no close family in the New World other than Uncle Rudolf, who was having difficulties of his own trying to establish a place for himself and his wife and daughter. Some of our distant relatives had either moved from the addresses my parents could find for them or simply chose to ignore and not answer our urgent inquiries. During all of this, time kept getting shorter.

My father eventually contacted someone in England who suggested that we go there to await our turn to immigrate into the United States. An immigration quota number was issued to everyone who wanted to enter the United States, and only when that number was called could that person obtain a visa. It was a different era, and at the time of the Holocaust no exceptions were made to the immigration quotas to allow desperate people whose lives

were in danger to escape and find a safe haven in this country.
Meanwhile, the Nazi government closed in on the Jews. All Jews were issued special identification, which included a passport-like document that had to be carried at all times and a large, yellow star of David that was always to be worn prominently on the chest. Middle names were not a popular custom among German Jews, but every Jewish man was required to assume the middle name Israel and every woman was given the middle name Sarah. Although most Jews generally accepted this practice with distaste as a form of insult and dropped these designations after the war, I began as soon as I was old enough to understand its significance to use the middle initial "S". I still employ it today as part of my name and wear it with pride, like a medal—or maybe more like a chip on my shoulder.

Economically, things were also bad. Jewish owned businesses were taken over without recompense by the Nazis, including my father and grandfather's factory. Bank accounts and any real estate other than primary residences were confiscated. The number of Jews hauled away to places like Dachau and Auschwitz increased, as did the pervasive and all-encompassing atmosphere of terror.

My father had just about given up with trying to find a sponsor in the United States when one day a scrawled letter arrived from a remote second cousin in San Francisco who had grudgingly agreed to supply the necessary guarantee. In return he expected my father to work in his cooperage business. If I had been old enough then to read and comprehend the letter I would have understood it to mean that my father would become as close to being an indentured servant as the law would allow—and possibly even a little closer.

On and off there was some talk of emigrating to Hong Kong, if not to South America, to await the calling of our number that would permit us to enter the United States. There were warnings that we would not be able to take much money or other valuables out of Germany. I am not sure exactly when and how the decision was made that we would go to England to wait, but I assume that the reasons included having to learn only one new language rather than two. We also had a distant relative in London, but I don't know if that had anything to do with our choice. In any case, one tearful day my mother and father and I said good-bye to my grandparents and great aunt and uncle. With no more than what we wore and could carry, we boarded a train for Holland.

There were so many soldiers and other uniformed men everywhere, and it seemed that each of them demanded to see our papers, which were examined with fear inspiring demeanor. Even to my seven and a half year old mind it was obvious that each of these requests brought about an additional sense of dread that something would be found amiss and we would be refused passage. I think even then I understood that a return to our home would mean immediate consignment to one of the concentration camps without any further possibility of release or escape.

Once we had reached Holland, the uniforms were much fewer, and those who wore them seemed considerably friendlier. From there the journey continued in the form of a very rough channel crossing by boat, which was my first experience on the water. We had a tiny cabin with narrow, uncomfortable bunks. None of us could sleep. What I remember most vividly of it was that my father was very quiet and nearly expressionless, a state that was to become the norm for the remaining quarter century of his life. My mother, on the other hand, was nearly hysterical; and I vomited almost nonstop all the way to England.

```
Der Leiter der Deutschen Volks-         Rottenburg,den 15.Novb.1938
schule in Rottenburg a.N.
Tgb.Nr.69o  Z.V,1
Herrn
      Siegfried .........B a u e r,Kaufmann
                                              in  R o t t e n b u r g
                                                                  a.N.
                                              Mechthildstr.32
        Nach einem Erlaß des Herrn Reichsministers Rust sind mit soforti-
   ger Wirkung alle jüdischen Schüler zu entlassen aus den deutschen
   Schulen;sie dürfen nur jüdische Schulen besuchen.
        Ihre Tochter L i l i a n,geb.2.8./31 ist somit ab heute nicht mehr
   Schülerin der allgemeinen Pflichtvolksschule.Weitere gesetzliche Re-
   gelung über ferneren Schulbesuch wird folgen.
                             Der Schulleiter:  Petzel
```

This is the official letter sent to my father in 1938 by the director of the Public School in Rottenburg telling him that Jewish children were no longer allowed to attend German schools. Since there were no Jewish schools in Rottenburg, my school days that I had enjoyed so much were over.

CHAPTER TWO

SEX EDUCATION

At some point between the ages of seven and a half and eight, on a cold and lonely Saturday morning in the lavatory of my nearly deserted school in the slum section of London's Camden Town, I learned the rudiments of the facts about the birds and bees.

It has to be understood that I am the daughter of a woman who was raised to be a Jewish princess, and a German Jewish princess at that. German Jewish princesses from the first half of the Twentieth Century did not teach their daughters many facts of life—at least not before they had learned most of them from another source. Early mother/daughter sex education did not go any further than, "Don't look at it, don't touch it and don't let anyone else." Oh, there was the ubiquitous, "Don't talk to strangers. Don't go with strange men." There were never any why's or wherefore's. German Jewish upbringing precluded ever asking why when it came to anything even remotely connected with sex.

The year we spent in London was undoubtedly one of the most painful and traumatic periods of my life. We were not completely destitute, but we were forced to live as if we were. Consequently, my parents rented the cheapest living quarters they could find, an upstairs bed sitter in Camden Town, a part of London that has in recent years become a trendy area. In 1939 it was mostly the domain of lower working class families and others of scant to very modest means.

Our cold and cheerless room was actually quite large, but it was sparsely furnished with just the bare necessities—three beds (one of them, no more than a cot, discreetly placed behind a dusty screen as far away from the other two, which were pushed close together, as possible); a standing wardrobe; a small and nondescript table; and some straight backed chairs that had seen better days. There was a fireplace in the middle of one of the long walls, opposite the door to the hallway and kitchen that was common to all of the rooms on that floor. An ancient toilet sat nestled in a curtained cubbyhole in one corner. There must have been a lamp or two, but they were probably nothing out of the ordinary, as I have no recollection at all of them. Possibly there was just a utilitarian ceiling light. I remember the room as being dark and gloomy both night and day.

    I was enrolled in a school about three blocks away, and I dutifully walked there five days a week, even in the soggy coldness of the London winter. It was difficult for me to follow what was going on in the classes, not only because I knew very little English in those days but also because I had missed a large part of my early schooling after the Nazis had decreed that Jewish children were no longer entitled to government provided education. There had been no Jewish schools in our little town, and my grandfather's efforts to teach me at home had been rudimentary at best, while they lasted. English schools were quite advanced. I tried very hard, especially since I had been thoroughly grounded in the theory that education is of the utmost importance. My young brain had already been struggling with that concept, particularly in light of my unceremonious ejection from public school in Germany after less than a year of study. School had been one of the wonders of the world to my young and untainted mind, and being suddenly and without much explanation ousted had been a terribly cruel blow. I don't believe that I had been made fully aware of why it had happened. Either my mother and my grandparents were still reeling from the shock of my father's abduction—the expulsion occurred during the two months that he was imprisoned in Dachau—or they simply felt that I would not be able to comprehend the school situation. In any case, there had been little talk about it. I think the omission was a bad mistake, as my utter turmoil at not knowing exactly why I had been expelled probably helped to form the tormenting roots of insecurity that have plagued me all of my life.

    Most formidable during the hostile year we spent in England, however, was the prospect of trying to fit in, to make friends, to actually become a viable part of my new life. The obstacles seemed quite insurmountable.

First there was the language barrier. Then there were the cultural differences. The children of Camden Town were tough little Cockneys with an attitude. I understood neither their heavily accented speech nor their ways. Poverty and lack of social skills ran rampant in that time and place. My parents had their own problems, which they attempted to conceal from me but the raw edges of which confronted me on an almost nonstop basis.

There were those that had been left behind. My grandparents and great aunt and uncle had refused to try to emigrate. They were too old, they said, and they felt that their social and financial position in their small, country town would leave them in a fairly safe place, especially when they considered my father's earlier release from Dachau after the greasing of a palm or two. They were so wrong, and I am sure at this point that my mother and father knew that all along, particularly my father, who had seen first hand the terrible things of which the Nazi hate machine was capable. My mother always went along with what he said, and his by then nearly constant state of dejection had dragged her down with him into a similar melancholy.

There was also the matter of money. Although my father had lost nearly everything in the German version of the post World War I depression, he had worked very diligently and had accrued a second comfortable amount of property and assets. My mother's family had always been quite well to do, and my mother had never wanted for anything. We had always had servants, until, about the same time that I was thrown out of school, the Nazi government had decreed that Aryans could not work for Jews. Our last cook and housekeeper had left several months before we boarded the train on our way to England.

Now we were in a strange country and were living hand to mouth, much like the peasant farmers to whom we had always given our cast-off clothing and often gifts of money. There was no way of knowing if we would ever be reunited with either the family we had left behind or with any of our property or other resources.

My parents did not learn English as readily as I, although they worked at it constantly from several home study courses. They were very proud people and did not want to have any more contact than absolutely necessary with our wealthy distant relative who lived in an upscale suburb of London. As far as I can remember, we visited Toni only once during our stay in England, when she had sent a car and driver for us. Most of the time we kept pretty much to ourselves.

Although school days in London were difficult, the most terrible time was the weekend. There was nothing for an eight year old with no friends and no money to do. The dingy bed sitter was cold and depressing, and I felt left out even from the conversations of my mother and father. It was obvious to me, even as young as I was, that they often wished to discuss matters they did not consider suitable for my ears. They would tell me to sit on my bed and read, or they would suggest I go out on the street to see if I could find the neighbors' calico cat, which I had grown to love as my best friend.

Frequently the long haired calico would be sitting on the outside steps of the house in which we lived, and I would sit down beside her and stroke her for hours, fantasizing that I could understand her purred words and that she understood what I told her. Occasionally, when she was not there, I would walk up or down the street looking for her. Sometimes I would walk as far as the schoolyard and stand watching the children play games that I did not understand. They rarely spoke to me—not even my classmates who knew who I was. Once or twice a girl invited me to join in a game of jump rope; but I did not know the rules, and even then I was clumsy and, I suppose, not much fun. They soon tired of me and told me I was "out". From necessity I learned how to be an aware observer.

One Saturday morning I ventured onto the play area and stood watching several groups of children. I have no recollection of what my thoughts might have been, but I know that they were not happy ones. They seldom were. Home was not a happy place either, so I had no desire to go back there. Eventually nature called and I walked over to the girls' lavatory, which was to the left of the school building. One of the older girls from my class was in the washroom. I knew her slightly because she was the biggest girl in the class and was probably a year or two older than the other students. She had most likely failed at her lessons and was behind one or more grades. She had been watching the door.

"Oh, it's th' German girl," she said as I came in.

I had the distinct impression that something strange was going on, but I had no idea what or even why I had such a feeling.

"Ye carnt come in 'ere," the girl said.

I must have looked quite puzzled, and I certainly had no idea what to say.

"D'ye 'ave any money?" the eleven year old asked.

I began to get worried. Why did she want to know? I shook my head. "No," I replied quite truthfully.

"Did ye know we wuz in 'ere?"

I could barely understand her through the heavy Cockney accent. I shook my head again, although I had no idea what she meant by "we." I was becoming increasingly frightened.

"Ye don' know nuthin'?" she asked.

I looked nervously toward the door, thinking maybe I didn't have to go to the bathroom after all and maybe I should leave. I was much too shy to speak up and tell her why I had come in.

The girl grabbed my arm. "Ye ever do it?" she asked.

I must have looked completely puzzled. I was.

She turned me loose. "Ye know, 'IT,'" she said. "Wha' a boy an' a girl do to get a bybee."

I had no idea what she was talking about, but somehow I knew that there was something wrong with it. I wanted to leave, but I also felt a budding curiosity. This conversation was treading on previously totally unfamiliar ground as far as I was concerned.

"Eh, ye sure ye ain't got no money?" Her attitude was not unfriendly. These kids understood lack of funds very well.

I stuck my hands into my pockets, pulled them out and made the universal gesture for empty.

"We been gettin' a penny to watch 'em do it," she said, indicating one of the toilet cubicles that had its door shut. She went on to explain that another girl from my class whose name has escaped me and an older boy named Peter were in the closed cubicle performing the sex act. Many children were very happy to pay a penny for the privilege of observing the action. For "tuppence" Peter would do it to other girls who wanted to learn, and for a "haypenny more" the girl in the cubicle would allow other boys to do it to her.

I was horrified. I had never heard of such an act, but from the very ambiance of the situation I knew that it must be one of those forbidden things to which my mother had sometimes alluded. Anyhow, it sounded disgusting. I could not understand why anyone would be willing to pay for this, either to watch it being done—or even why anyone would want to do it.

"I tell ye wha," the girl went on. "We'll let ye watch, an' if ye bring some money next time Peter'll show ye how t' do it."

Before I could protest, she led me over to the cubicle and told them to unlock the door. I wanted to leave, but in some strange way I was fascinated. I was about to learn something verboten, and the idea had a strange and rather magnetic appeal.

It was many years later before I fully understood what I had seen that Saturday morning—and that it was actually a very fragmentary part of what had been advertised as "the" sex act. In the crowded confines of the toilet cubicle stood Peter, a grimy, somewhat simple boy of maybe twelve or thirteen, and an unkempt little girl of nine or ten. She had her skirt up and the crotch of her panties pulled aside, while Peter, who, I suppose, was aptly named, touched her with something that he had cupped in his grubby hands, something that seemed to be attached inside his unbuttoned shorts. I looked at the two of them only briefly before turning away. I had not seen a great deal, but the squalid diorama shall undoubtedly remain graphically in my mind forever.

CHAPTER THREE

MR. THOMAS

In the course of a lifetime we all meet a few truly unforgettable people. Some of these individuals may leave with us something indelible that in some way, either good or bad, impacts a part of our very being for an entire lifetime. Mr. Thomas certainly fits into this category, although it was not until many years later that I fully realized what this strange but kindly man had done for me.

When my parents and I fled from Germany in 1939 we went to England with our quota number to await permission to enter the United States. We had no idea how long we would have to remain in the UK, and our situation was financially most precarious. Unable to take with us anything beyond what we were able to wear and carry, we had little money and no means of obtaining more. British law at that time prohibited temporary residents from gainful employment. To make matters worse, my parents spoke almost no English and were totally ignorant of the ways and wiles of our host country. In order to conserve money, we took up residence in a rooming house in London's Camden Town, then a shabby neighborhood of low income working people bordering on being a slum area.

The house consisted of three floors of "bed sitter" rooms, a basement flat and a loft apartment that was occupied by the building's owner or manager, whom we knew as Mr. Thomas. There was a community kitchen on each floor that was shared by the residents of the individual rooms on that level. A single full bath with an ancient metal tub on curved, rusty legs was located on the middle story for the use of everyone who lived in all the bed sitters in the entire house. Each room had its own toilet, just barely hidden away in a cubbyhole with a skimpy curtain hanging on rings from a wooden rod to afford some small semblance of privacy.

Some of the tenants were singles but most were husband and wife. At the time my parents and I resided in the building we were the only unit of three, and Mr. Thomas had provided a cot for my use. The basement belonged to a policeman and his wife, who were a cut above the rest of the renters in financial and, therefore, social status.

Our room was fairly large and reasonably clean; but, like the others, had no means of heating other than the fireplace. I think my lack of enthusiasm about the romantic aspects of having a fireplace dates back to those freezing cold Winter months in London when the only way to keep warm was to stand before the fire and alternately bake one's front or behind while one's flip side threatened to turn to ice.

We led an existence that was as dreary as the London weather. My parents were ill equipped emotionally to cope with what was happening to them. For the most part they did little besides observe the sorry state of their crumbled world, and they worried constantly about the relatives and friends that we had left behind in Germany. My entertainment consisted of mostly failed attempts to join the closed corporations of my Cockney schoolmates and of playing with the long haired calico cat that belonged to one of the neighbors and which I thought was the most beautiful and wonderful creature on the face of the earth. An occasional walk in the park or a window shopping excursion through Woolworth's offered an infrequent extraordinary recreational treat for my parents and me. There was no television to fall back on in those days, and we had no money for movies or other diversions. We did not even own a radio.

Most of the residents of the rooming house kept pretty much to themselves. Whether this was from suspicion toward the foreigners or because it was simply their nature I really do not know even to this day; but the end result was the same—a constant feeling of loneliness and isolation. My mother and father had each other, but I felt alone and alienated and could not completely understand why my life should have taken this turn.

I had seen Mr. Thomas on several occasions, and I frequently overheard my parents discussing him, usually in hushed voices. I did not grasp the meaning of their conversation then. When I think back now, I remember Mr. Thomas as a man probably in his mid or late thirties, although to an eight year old he looked to be of indeterminate but probably elderly years. He was tall and slender and had a thin, dark mustache. If years and imagination don't betray me, he looked a little like Errol Flynn. Soft spoken and polite, Mr. Thomas seemed to be a night person. He always came down the stairs from the attic toward evening, when darkness began to fall. He left the house almost nightly, and I never saw or heard him return. He went out sometimes during the day as well, but when he did that it was usually only briefly. The thing about Mr. Thomas that sent tongues wagging, although in my childish naiveté I could see nothing bizarre about it, was that when he went out at night he always wore lipstick and makeup—enough of the latter to cover his mustache. He was given to wearing long, heavy overcoats and frequently during winter he sported a tremendous, nearly ankle length fur.

Mr. Thomas rarely failed to exchange an amiable greeting with my parents and almost always had a few kind words for me. I grew very fond of him and must have seen him in my fantasies as something of a knight in shining armor. Occasionally I dreamed about him in that context. Even at that tender age I was quite aware that when people whispered things behind a person's back it was usually something ugly, and I failed to comprehend why anyone would want to say bad things about "my" Mr. Thomas.

One day Mr. Thomas knocked on our door when he was on his way out. He spoke to my mother in his usual subdued, somewhat diffident manner. Like many children who have become accustomed to being left out of things, I had developed extremely acute hearing and the habit of carefully eavesdropping. To my boundless delight Mr. Thomas was asking my mother whether he might take me to the cinema to see the new Disney production that was creating such a sensation in London—"Fantasia". He explained that it was a magnificent film that was filled with great music presented in a manner that would appeal to young children and perhaps develop in them an appreciation for the classics. He was careful not to intimate that perhaps my parents might be financially unable or otherwise unwilling to supply this treat for their little daughter.

Of course I perked up with joy at the very idea. I had never in my life been to a movie and could only let my wildest imagination run rampant to tell me what it would be like—especially to go with my handsome knight. It was as if I had been struck down by a lightning bolt when I heard my mother, in her halting English, politely turn down the invitation. I was absolutely crushed in spite of hearing Mr. Thomas say, "Please think about it. It's a marvelous film and all children should see it. The music is absolutely outstanding. I've already seen it twice myself."

After Mr. Thomas had left, I asked why I couldn't go. It was something my mother did not wish to explain to me, and in her rigid old world way there was never any need to supply a child with a reason. I knew full well that to pursue the issue was to appear to be questioning her authority, which would most likely result in a slap across the face or even more severe punishment. However, thanks to our cramped living quarters I overheard the ensuing discussion between my parents. Although I am not able to recall it word for word, it went, of course in German, something like this:

"Mr. Thomas wants to take Lilian to the theater."

"That's nice of him."

"I told him no."

"Why not?"

"Why not? The man is a freak. Who knows what he might do or what terrible things she might learn from him."

"Don't be silly, Trude. He is what he is, and he isn't interested in little girls. He's just trying to be nice."

I believe that my mother was not at all convinced by my father's explanation, but most of the time she yielded to his point of view. My father had traveled extensively. At one time involved in the millinery business, he had spent quite some time in Paris, and he had seen more than a little of life in all of its varieties. He was also a man of superior intellect. In any case, it does not matter what my mother may or may not have thought. It was thanks to my father that I was allowed to go out with Mr. Thomas.

We went to see "Fantasia," parts of which I absorbed with all the wide-eyed wonder a guileless eight year old can engender. Some parts of the film were beyond my comprehension, and my limited command of English in those days was not enough to allow me to understand much of the dialogue. The fabulous sound track, however, as Mr. Thomas had suggested might happen, set off in me the first spark of a life-long passion for classical music. He and I mutually agreed to sit through the film one and a half times, as in those days motion pictures were shown continuously and one could remain in the theater as long as one wished. We would have stayed to see all of it twice, but Mr. Thomas was afraid to bring me home too late. He still wanted to take me for an ice cream, since I had told him that I had eaten ice cream only once before, when I was about five or six years old. It was a marvelous and wondrous evening, the memory of which enhanced and sometimes even replaced the mundane reality of my day to day existence for quite some time afterward.

When we returned to the rooming house and I thanked him profusely, Mr. Thomas told me that he, too, had enjoyed the outing and that we would have to do it again soon. However, not long thereafter England entered the war and all school-aged children, including myself, were evacuated to the country for safety from the impending blitz. I returned to London only shortly before our departure for America, and the opportunity for another magical outing with Mr. Thomas did not arise.

It was likely that Mr. Thomas went off to the war and, like so many others, did not return. In any case, I never saw him again and once we were a continent away we lost all touch with the people we had known in London. I hope that he survived the war and that he found whatever kind of happiness he sought. In a world gone awry, he had been a breath of sweetness and kindness in my life, and I am certain that he is responsible for much of the compassion and empathy I am able to feel for others, not to mention my anger when I encounter senseless prejudice. More than that, he taught me something very significant—not to form judgments by the way people look or dress or talk—nor to fault them if they appear to be different from the accepted so-called norm.

This photo of my sandbox in Rottenburg, Germany was taken in 1936, before my friends were persuaded to stop playing with me. I'm second from the left, wearing the big bow in my hair.

CHAPTER FOUR

STEEPLE MORDEN

As soon as Great Britain joined in the war against Germany the British government took precautions to guard the nation's children from the inevitable air strikes on London. Plans were quickly in place to evacuate all school aged children from areas that were most likely to be attacked. No time was lost in contacting farmers and other country residents asking them to take in as many city children as possible.

Such an effort is probably difficult for most Americans to understand. Distance formed a great ally for the United States during World War II, but England was located about an hour's flying time from Germany even in the days of propeller powered planes early in the war, before the advent of jets. The crowded residential areas of London could easily have become death traps for many thousands of innocent children. The British government was well aware of that possibility and encouraged London families to send their children away for the duration.

Within days of the declaration of war notices went out through the schools to all parents that their children would be sent to live in the country, where they would hopefully be out of range of the expected Luftwaffe bombing raids. The evacuation was semi-voluntary. Much pressure was put upon parents to send their offspring to where they would reside in relative safety. The government paid the cost of transportation and would give the host families a small monthly stipend to pay for the room and board of the youngsters they took in.

I definitely did not want to go. I was desperately lonely and unhappy in London, but at least I was with my parents, and the neighbors' beloved calico cat was there most of the time to listen to me pour out my problems. The idea of living with complete strangers in what was already a strange country terrified me. I think I even, in my immature mind, equated the decision of my parents to force me to go with their wanting to get rid of me. After all, I was painfully aware that the bed sitter was very crowded, and none of us had the privacy to which we had been accustomed while still living in Germany.

My mother was very definite in insisting that I should go. The British government had said it was best for the children, and nothing in her makeup allowed her to believe that the leaders of our temporary haven could be wrong. I think my father had some inkling of understanding my reluctance, but like most European men he nearly always deferred to the mother in matters of dealing with the child—especially a female child.

The relationship between my mother and me had begun to deteriorate shortly after our arrival in London—possibly even before. She had always been given to requiring blind and instant obedience to her demands, which I had learned at an early age never to question. German children were accustomed to discipline, and a parent's word was law, with never a need for explanation. One just did what one was told. Children learned quickly not to ask why. Yet, when the world into which I had been born and had always known had begun to crumble, along with it went my sense of security. I had begun occasionally to display what in those days was known as a temper tantrum. Today's child psychologists would call this "acting out". The way in which my mother always put an end to these demonstrations was the swift and potent application of her hand to the seat of my pants, followed by a severe tongue-lashing. If I really overstepped the boundaries of what was considered proper behavior for a small child, which in my case usually meant speaking my mind, the application of the hand would be even more swift and generally across my face.

The occasion of my departure for the train that would take me from London to the country village of Steeple Morden triggered one of the worst of these scenes. I refused to get out of bed that morning and after being physically dragged from under the covers

I dawdled miserably with brushing my teeth and putting on my clothes.

"You're such a stubborn child," my mother said sternly. "If you behave like that no one will like you. No wonder you don't have any friends."

I had never explained to my mother that the friends that were available to me included pre-teens who performed perfunctory sex acts in the girls' lavatory for other children to watch for a fee of pennies.

My parents had never visited my school. A neighbor who spoke English had offered to take me there for the necessary registration, a proposal they had gratefully accepted. There were never any questions about my teachers or my schoolmates and very little talk about my curriculum and how, or if at all, I might be coping. My parents were almost totally preoccupied with their current plight and with the looming prospective of a very uncertain future.

"I don't want to go," I kept saying petulantly. "I won't know anyone there. Everyone else has a brother or sister going with them, and they can stay together. Why don't I have a brother or sister?"

"The stork never sent us one," my mother would reply.

I accepted that answer, but it still failed to tell me why. As I was growing up in Germany, before the trouble started, it had never made much difference; but in England, where I was so alone and alienated, I truly felt that I had been cheated by not having a sibling.

My mother packed my suitcase and my rucksack, or backpack, both of which were German and, like my clothes, would brand me as a foreigner even before I could open my mouth to verbally identify myself as such. She put a few chocolate candies in the backpack and told me that they were a special treat and not to eat them all at once. Such treats had become a very infrequent and therefore great luxury.

My father was to take me to the train. My mother hugged and kissed me and told me that I should be good and that I should write at least once a week.

Steeple Morden was, I suppose, a typical small English farming village, consisting of little more than a church, a school house, a small shop that sold textiles and general merchandise that included a few grocery items, a tiny railway station and a few crumbling, very old cottages. Produce was sold by individual farmers as it was harvested. The roughly paved streets extended to country roads that radiated out toward a few scruffy farms. Many years later I would have applied to Steeple Morden the term "picturesque," but at the age of eight I saw it only as ugly, dismal and forlorn.

As I recall, the train ride from London was about two hours. I have no idea in which direction we went, and I have been unable to locate Steeple Morden on any of the maps to which I have access, including the Britannica World Atlas. As a matter of fact, until quite recently I thought the name of the town was Steeple Morton, a name I could not find listed anywhere when I began to look for it. I eventually found a listing on the Internet for a Steeple Morden, so that is most likely the correct spelling of the name for the place to which I was sent so many years ago.

Several teachers accompanied the large number of children and did their best to keep us reasonably quiet and out of mischief during the ride. We had been given hand-lettered name badges to wear for identification during our exodus from London, and I immediately had begun to think about those yellow stars we had been forced to wear.

It was not at all difficult for me to remain silent. I was sandwiched among some younger evacuees from another school. I watched the scenery speed by and slowly allowed the hypnotic, mechanical clickety-clack of the wheels going over the rails to replace the unhappy images that filled my mind. I had been told only that I was going to the country for my own good, that I would be safer there than in London. No time element had been mentioned, and I wondered whether I was to be separated from my family forever. I dwelled on that possibility so much that there was no room for pondering what the immediate future held in store.

At Steeple Morden a group of shabbily dressed people awaited the arrival of our train. As we climbed down, some of them examined our name tags and read the names aloud. As each was announced, someone would come through the crowd to claim the child. I learned later that many of the local farmers were completely illiterate.

The woman who came for me had a tanned, wrinkled face and looked to me to be almost as old as my grandmother. She was actually a few years younger than my mother. Her features were regular and not unattractive, but her demeanor was severe and humorless and her expression was one of weariness. Her dress was plain and dark—blue or black and dully nondescript. The dark brown hair was stringy and graying. She was not a large woman, but she appeared to be strong. She identified herself and said that she was to be my guardian. She spoke in a dialect that was unfamiliar to me but not as difficult to understand as the Cockney accent I had heard so much in Camden Town.

"They told me you don't speak much English," she said as she took my suitcase and began to lead me away from the other children.

I clung to my knapsack and said nothing.

"You're shy too," she continued. It sounded as if she intended it to be criticism or possibly a complaint, but I was not sure.

"Do you know anything about living on a farm?"

I shook my head.

"I'm Mrs. Harker. We 'ave an apple orchard and some pears, and we raise chickens too—for eggs."

She scribbled something in a book that one of the accompanying teachers was holding, mumbled a few words, then suggested that I should follow her.

We walked away from the railway station, which was located on an unpaved road. Soon the road narrowed and turned into more of a path rather than a road. There were vague ruts that indicated that an occasional vehicle had passed that way, but for the most part we walked along what appeared to be a brown ribbon flanked by endless fields of some sort of grain. It became increasingly difficult for me to keep up with the woman's brisk pace.

"Come along, child. We don't 'ave all day," Mrs. Harker said gruffly. "There's lots of work to do on the farm."

I speeded up as much as I could.

"You're what—eight years old?"

"Yes. In August."

For a moment she was silent. Then she said, "That's old enough. You're going to take care of my little girl, Eleanor. Make sure she don't get in no trouble."

At that point I had no idea what she meant, but it soon became painfully apparent that this family had signed up to take in a city child not only for the extra money but because they wanted a free live-in baby-sitter. That was one of the multitude of things with which I had absolutely no experience.

After what seemed an endless walk—it was about half an hour—we arrived at the Harker farm, which consisted of what appeared to be infinite, slightly ragged rows of trees. A dingy looking stone and wood farmhouse peeked out from among them. There was a vaguely overgrown path that led from the road to the house and the ramshackle outbuildings that stood to one side and behind it. An equally depressing and dilapidated wooden fence surrounded the property, the sagging gate standing partially open. Nothing about it appeared in any way inviting.

"There ain't no animals to run off," said Mrs. Harker, "So we ain't fixed the fence. Chickens can't get out of their yard."

The Harkers, I learned later, did not own the property or much of anything else. They were tenant farmers who eked out a bare living from the apples, pears and eggs they could produce and sell. They also grew their own vegetables and kept an aging cow that sometimes gave them the milk they needed. There was no automated equipment in those days, and the interminable work of keeping the orchard going was done just by the two of them.

Mr. Harker, like his wife, looked much older than he really was. A lifetime of rigorous toil and harsh conditions had left their mark on both of them. In addition, Mr. Harker was prone to drowning his sorrows in whatever alcoholic drink was available, which added to his worn and haggard appearance.

On the inside the house, which was surprisingly large, appeared well scrubbed and clean, but it was sparsely furnished and cold both in appearance and in actual temperature.

As we walked through the door a pallid, thin little girl with stringy brown hair came skipping toward us.

"That's Ellie," said Mrs. Harker. "Ellie, this is Lilian. She's going to live with us for a while."

Ellie regarded me suspiciously.

"She's going to be taking care of you and watching you," Mrs. Harker went on.

Ellie gave me what I interpreted as an almost evil look.

"I ain't got time for foolishness," said Mrs. Harker to both of us. "Lilian, you're responsible. If Ellie don't be'ave, you'll get punished for it. You understand?"

I didn't understand. I had never heard of such an arrangement, and it just didn't sound right. How was I to see that this six year old girl with the insolent face would behave? Without fully realizing why, I was terrified.

"Now show Lilian your room," said Mrs. Harker. "I got work to do. Show 'er where to put 'er clothes." She handed me my suitcase.

I followed Ellie to a plainly furnished bedroom. It did not look like a child's room. There were no toys and no pictures, and the curtains and bedclothes were clean but colorless and drab. There was a double bed, a small freestanding wardrobe, a chest of drawers and a small table, like an end table, which looked as if it did not belong where it stood, next to the window. The wardrobe and chest were against the opposite wall. Everything was made of a heavy looking, darkish wood and bore the scratches and wear of many years of use.

Ellie pointed to the little table. "That's yours," she said succinctly.

I looked at the bed, realizing that in all likelihood I was going to have to share it with Ellie. The idea did not sit well with me. I had never slept in the same bed with anyone before.

"I suppose you're used to 'avin' your own room," said Ellie.

I made no reply.

"Well, I don't like it neither," she continued. "I didn't ask for you to come 'ere."

I just wanted to go home. Even the freezing cold, crowded London bed sitter was better than this.

"Can't you talk?" asked Ellie.

"I can talk."

"You talk funny."

"I am learning English. I speak German," I said.

"Say something in German," said Ellie, sounding a little more childlike than before.

I was too shy to oblige.

"Come on," she urged. "Tell me how to say 'kiss my bum' in German."

I had never heard that word. "I do not know what is bum," I admitted.

Ellie laughed derisively. "You're dumb," she said. "You don't know where your bum is."

The little waif of a girl stood watching me. Her eyes darted from my suitcase, which I had placed on the floor in front of the narrow table, to my backpack, which now reposed on top of it.

"Ain't you going to put your stuff away?" she finally asked. "You can use 'alf of one of my drawers." She waved a hand in the direction of the chest.

I did not want to start unpacking my things, hoping against hope that this was all a big mistake and my parents would suddenly appear to take me away from this place.

Ellie gave my suitcase a swift kick, and I had the thought that she was soon going to do the same to my shins. I was quite aware that Ellie was very curious about the contents of my baggage and that she probably would laugh at my strange looking, foreign clothing and underwear. I already did not like this child.

Mrs. Harker burst into the room at that point and quickly assessed the scene. Without a word she scooped up my suitcase, set it on the bed and opened it. Then she proceeded to put my few neatly folded sweaters, skirts and underthings into one of the drawers in the chest. There were still a few small items in the bag, but she slammed it shut and deposited it on the floor between the wardrobe and the chest.

"Don't be late for supper," she said dourly and swiftly walked out of the room.

I did not unpack or even open my other bag, which contained the candies, school supplies, some handkerchiefs and a small Steiff cat that had been my favorite toy as long as I could remember.

Ellie stuck her little hand into her crotch, glanced at me to make sure that she had my attention, and said, "That's my bum."

Over the next few days I learned many other words that I had not heard before either in English or even in German. Ellie had an amazing and colorful vocabulary for a six year old and what appeared to me to be a frightening knowledge of the facts of life. She imparted much of it on me as we lay side by side in the bed, often enlisting the visual aid of lifting her flannel nightgown to show me what she meant. I was too naive to understand half of it. It often took me a long time after Ellie had drifted away to sleep to shut off my own racing mind. I not only disliked this little girl, but I was also afraid of her.

That was not the only issue that kept me awake well into the night. I was learning first hand about the hard and unrelenting life of Great Britain's poor farmers.

There was never enough food to go around, for instance. Mr. Harker always ate his fill. Then Mrs. Harker made certain that Ellie was satisfied. She and I shared what remained, and I think my portion was often less than I would have liked. I instinctively knew not to ask for more, although there were many days when I was still hungry when I left the table.

One evening when the meal had been particularly scant I thought of the chocolates in my knapsack and decided to eat some of them to fill the empty spaces. When I opened my bag, I saw that the candy was gone.

When Ellie came into the room I questioned her.

She shrugged her narrow shoulders.

"Those were my chocolate. You took them," I said angrily.

"Didn't."

"I tell your mother."

"She won't believe you."

Ellie was right. I went in search of Mrs. Harker, and when I found her—she was in the kitchen—I told her what Ellie had done. She shouted at me that she had not taught her daughter to steal or to lie. She warned me not to come to her again accusing Ellie of such wrongdoing.

I was both mortified and frightened. The way things looked, Ellie could do anything to me and I would have no recourse. I did the only thing I knew to do. I wrote to my parents and told them about the situation at the Harkers. I said I wanted to come home.

My schooling in Germany had been so brief that I had never really learned to write properly in German; so my letters were written in a combination of the two languages. I wrote every two or three days, each time begging fervently for my parents to come and get me.

Several weeks went by, and I heard nothing from my mother and father. Beyond my own discomfort and unhappiness I began to worry that something had happened to them. They had promised to write.

My responsibility for Ellie's behavior laid a heavy burden on an already troubled eight year old. Ellie teased and tormented me with threats of doing terrible things for which I would receive the blame if I even thought of telling her parents about any of her outrageous actions. Every day I walked with her to and from school, which was a nearly forty-five minute walk each way. At school, although we were not in the same class, Ellie was always nearby. A few times I had it in mind to tell a teacher that I was not getting enough to eat and that I was worried because I had not heard from my parents, but I could not find a private moment without my despicable little shadow.

Ellie constantly mocked my accent and taunted me about one thing or another. In retrospect I think she probably liked me and this was her way of showing her feelings. At the time, I thought she really hated me. She always dallied on the way home from school, causing us both to be late, for which I was berated on a nearly daily basis.

The weeks passed, and I heard nothing. I kept writing regularly, handing Mrs. Harker the sealed letters, which she said she would post. The blossoms on the trees in the orchard turned to fruit, and soon there were little green apples by the thousands. Each day they grew larger.

One day Ellie was particularly slow on the way home, and nothing I could say to her would speed her up. She climbed fences, petted dogs, chased loose chickens and ducks and danced backwards and forwards in skipping little steps along the road—all of which delayed us further. When we reached the Harker house the evening meal was already on the table, and Mrs. Harker was livid.

"I'm tired of telling you not to bring 'er 'ome so late," she shouted at me. "You go on to bed without supper."

I knew by then that argument was useless. Dejectedly I went to our room while Ellie giggled at the table.

I wrote another letter. My empty stomach was growling, and I knew that I would not be able to sleep unless I could get something into it.

By then I had learned very well the unvarying habits of the senior Harkers. Knowing that they were busy with their meal, I quietly tiptoed out of the room and out through the front door, staying as far from the dining room/kitchen area as possible.

There was still some daylight, and I made my way down the path until I was reasonably sure I could not be seen from the house.

I left the walkway and moved a little into the depth of the orchard. There I picked an apple and sat under the tree from which it had come and ate my stolen fruit. It was not quite ripe and still very hard, but my teeth were good and my stomach was grateful. I must have picked and eaten three or four more apples before I wiped my mouth carefully with my handkerchief and made my way back to the house.

Luck was with me. The Harkers were still at the table, and I was able to sneak back into the bedroom without being noticed. I undressed quickly and quietly and got into bed. I was asleep by the time Ellie came in.

At some time during the night—it was pitch dark and Ellie was sleeping beside me—I was rudely awakened by the result of my green apple feast. I had horrible stomach cramps and an excruciatingly urgent need to get to the bathroom quickly. Unfortunately, the Harker bathroom was quite a long distance from where I slept. I had no time to ruminate on whether it would be more prudent to try to make a run for it or to lie still with my buttocks clamped tightly together, hoping that the feeling would pass. Diarrhea as I had never known it before struck suddenly and forcefully, and I could do nothing to stop it.

When it was over, I did my best, in the dark, to try to clean myself and the bed with whatever I could find—some sheets of writing paper and a handkerchief. The mess was really awful, and I was in a panic. I was quite sure that Mrs. Harker was going to kill me when she found the soiled bedding and no matter how hard I tried there was nothing I could do to repair the damage or to hide it. There was no nearby access even to cold running water.

In the morning, when there was enough daylight, I tried to make up my side of the bed to conceal my shame. Ellie was still asleep but not for long. Once awake, she lost no time in running to get her mother to show her what I had done.

To say that Mrs. Harker was infuriated would be putting it mildly. The image of her arm-waving and shouting of loud epithets that I mostly did not understand remained with me for a very long time. She must have called me everything her limited vocabulary could call forth from filthy to imbecilic. Many were words I had never heard before.

I was so completely terrified that I did something I knew even as I did it to be totally preposterous. I denied having done this thing. Reverting to the reactions of a child half my age, I repeated several times that it had not been I who had dirtied the bed.

"So you're going to lie to me too," screamed Mrs. Harker. She slapped me so hard that I stumbled backwards. "I suppose you're going to say Ellie did it, you dirty, miserable Jew brat."

At first, before terror completely overcame me, I stammered that I had been so hungry that I knew I would not be able to sleep; so I had eaten several unripe apples.

"You filthy little thief," Mrs. Harker yelled at me. She grabbed my arm roughly and pulled me toward the bed.

I thought she was going to push my face into what remained of the fecal matter, but she suddenly released me and, almost violently, yanked the sheets from the bed.

"I should make you wash these," she said angrily, "but you'd better get on to school. We don't want Ellie to be late."

She stormed out of the room, carrying the crumpled up bedding, and slammed the door.

I was still shaking and petrified with fright when Ellie came into the room grinning from ear to ear. She made some impish remarks that bordered on nastiness and went about the business of dressing for school.

That night I wrote a very passionate letter to my mother and father in which I virtually begged them to come and get me. I did not want to speak to Mrs. Harker for any reason at all, so I decided I would take the letter with me to school and ask my teacher to mail it.

So much of the time I spent in Steeple Morden was traumatic that I must have tried to push that entire part of my life completely out of my mind. I have little idea exactly how long I resided with the Harkers. I know only that it seemed like an eternity, although it could not have been more than three or four months. It might have been only a few weeks.

A few days after the green apple incident, on a Saturday morning when there was no school, I received the surprise of my life. My mother appeared at the Harkers' front door.

Mr. Harker was working out in the orchard, and Ellie had gone off somewhere, possibly to play with one of the neighborhood children. Mrs. Harker greeted the visitor with astonishment.

When she learned who the unfamiliar woman was she did not look pleased, although she attempted to appear cordial. She invited my mother into the house.

My mother's English was extremely limited in those days. It was very difficult for her to explain the reason for her visit, but she got quickly to the point. She had received a letter from me in which there had been several indications that I was not only very unhappy but was possibly being mistreated.

Mrs. Harker disclaimed everything. "Your daughter tells fibs," she said without emotion. "We've given 'er a good 'ome 'ere."

Addressing me in German, my mother asked me if I had received the two packages that had been sent to me. Then she asked about the letters she had written.

I had received none of these, nor had any of my entreaties reached London until I had given my most recent one to someone other than Mrs. Harker to mail. My mother went on, still in German, to tell me that the two packages had contained cookies, candy and some warm winter underwear. All had been intercepted by the Harkers.

Mrs. Harker stood in silence as we spoke, the look on her face suggesting that she was probably aware of the subject matter of the conversation in spite of it being in a language she did not understand.

"I vant to talk alone vith Lilian," my mother said.

Mrs. Harker did not like the idea, but she nodded, turned and walked outside.

I led my mother into my room, all the while spouting alternately in English and German all the pent up heartache and trepidation of the past weeks. At first I thought she did not believe me, but I think her silence came out of anger rather than discredit.

She asked where my things were kept, and when I told her she got the suitcase out of the wardrobe, opened the drawer I had indicated and began to pack my clothes. There was no need for conversation or explanation. I knew that I would be going back to London with her, but as long as I was in the Harker house I dared not express nor even feel my joy.

It was only a few minutes before Mrs. Harker entered the room, understanding the scene at a glance. "'Ow dare you look in my drawers!" she shouted at my mother, her eyes blazing.

For a moment my mother stood in nonplused silence, regarding the woman's acrimonious face while she formulated what she would say next. I thought they might come to blows, and I was frightened. I was old enough to understand that Mrs. Harker probably had far more experience with physical violence than my mother did.

"I take my daughter home," my mother finally said sternly. Turning to me and speaking in German she told me to get my knapsack and anything else that belonged to me—and, for once, to do it quickly.

Mrs. Harker, seeing her monthly government check evaporate, suddenly became more gentle in her speech and expression. She tried to tell my mother that it was all a misunderstanding and that it would be much better if I stayed, that I would be safe from harm in case bombs should fall on London. I do not believe that my mother understood a good part of what Mrs. Harker was trying to explain, but I certainly did; and I was gladly willing to face the air attacks and whatever else the Nazis might throw at us rather than remain one more wretched day in this hell hole.

CHAPTER FIVE

AMERICA

EARLY IN 1940 our immigration quota number finally came up, and in March of that year we sailed from Southampton on the aging Cunard White Star liner, the SS Lancastria.

It was a cold, harsh and gloomy crossing. For almost the entire ten days the ocean was rough and forbidding, and the ship's motion kept my mother and me in an almost constant state of nausea. My father was physically well, but he cycled in and out of his deep depressions, during which he spoke only as much as was absolutely necessary. Later, as I grew older and more aware, I realized that he was a true depressive, and sometimes he would go days without uttering a single word while he was at home with my mother and me.

Our cabin was an inside one on one of the lower decks, and during the entire voyage it remained hot and stuffy. We shared a toilet with several other staterooms, and to get to it or to the dining room meant navigating long, dingy, institutionally cream colored passageways while holding onto the well worn railing that ran the length of the bulkheads. Unable because of the ongoing war to seek other, calmer seas, the ship lurched almost constantly on the ponderous waves. I still remember the odd feeling of picking up a foot and having the floor seem to come up to meet it before I could complete the step. There was always an unpleasant, pervasive odor in most of the ship's passageways. Later I understood that it consisted of a mixture of a strong disinfectant cleaning solution and recently spewed vomit.

My father, wearing his heaviest clothing, his perennial hat and a wool muffler wrapped about his neck, spent much solitary time on deck. My mother and I tried a few times to go with him to get some fresh air, but the frigid temperature, the damp spray and the gray, dismal sky and sea were too disagreeable. My father tried to convince me that I would feel better on deck, but watching the endless upheaval of the ocean while the Lancastria bobbed up and down seemingly helplessly made matters worse. I had the feeling of being a Lilliputian figure on a toy boat battling against an overpowering alien world that was made up of relentless, undulating monsters that threatened to swallow up my entire ship along with me.

The mandatory blackouts at night and daily lifeboat drills were frightening too. British ships were being randomly torpedoed in the North Atlantic, and the possibility of an air strike was ever present, even against a civilian transport—especially one known to be carrying Jewish refugees to the United States. In fact, the Lancastria, which shuttled regularly back and forth between the ports of Southampton and New York, was sunk by German fire on one of her next crossings.

My father kept trying to tell my mother and me that the food in the dining salon was excellent. After nearly a year of sketchy meals prepared in the community kitchen of our London quarters by my mother, who had never really learned how to cook, I suppose any kind of shipboard fare, even a bland English menu, would have appealed to him. Although my father had no more experience at sea than my mother and I, he was not at all subject to the motion sickness that remained with her and me almost constantly during the crossing. I could scarcely bear the overpowering odor of food that permeated the dining room without feeling the urge to throw up, and I ate very little.

The first land we saw was Halifax, Nova Scotia, where the Lancastria sailed briefly into port to unload a few passengers and some cargo. I was overjoyed to see the shoreline and completely crushed when told that we were not quite there yet and would have to endure another day and night of being at sea.

The sight of New York harbor evoked a complex combination of emotions in my parents that I was much too young and immature to understand. I did find our arrival very exciting—especially when the significance of the Statue of Liberty was explained to me.

Almost from the moment we stepped off the gangplank onto American soil I had a feeling of belonging that I had never experienced during the time we had spent in England. The air itself felt very different, and it felt good to draw in great lungfulls of it, although I was still a little unsteady on my feet after having been away so long from terra firma.

Once again, as we had done when leaving Germany, we traveled with only those belongings we could carry. The great steamer trunks that had been shipped to us in London had been only partially unpacked and then placed in storage. In preparation for our journey to the United States my parents had carefully repacked our things so that we would have to carry with us only what we needed for the ocean voyage and the train ride from the East Coast to California. The trunks were consigned directly to San Francisco, although their contents were carefully examined in customs on the pier. We stood by for what seemed like hours as agents compared the lists of declaration my parents had made with the items that were stored in the trunks.

Another lengthy delay occurred at Immigration, while several clerks made sure that our papers were completely in order. Finally the passports and visas were stamped, and we were on our way to the promised new life.

For some reason that either was not explained to me or I simply do not remember it was necessary for us to spend two days and two nights in New York City before proceeding on to the West coast. Someone in the immigration office recommended a cheap hotel not too far from Pennsylvania Station, from where our train for California was to leave. Knowing neither the language nor anything about local public transportation, we rode to the hotel in a taxi, and I stared out of the window in nearly breathless wonderment at the forest of skyscrapers that surrounded us. The skyline was completely unlike anything I had ever seen before, even in London. Both of my parents were very silent during the entire ride.

Someone at the hotel told my father about the Automat, and we ate our next few meals there. We still had to be extremely cautious about money, so the rather meager selections were made for me; but I was completely fascinated with the system, the likes of which I had never seen before or even imagined possible. As usual,

I ate very slowly; but this time it was not because of my tendency to dawdle. A great deal of my attention was devoted to watching the hordes of people put coins into the slots and subsequently remove their food.

I saw several items I wanted to try, but my mother said that I had already eaten enough. I was not actually hungry, but the mechanical procedure of selecting and acquiring anything from a banana or an apple to a slice of gooey pie or a bowl of soup held me completely transfixed. I think, had I been allowed to do so, I would have spent hours dropping in money and watching the varied fare emerge—even including items I normally abhorred.

The Automat was not the only novelty to catch my fancy. With little in the way of disposable cash and plenty of time to kill, especially in the evening when walking around unfamiliar Manhattan in the nippy March air held no appeal, we spent hours sitting in the lobby of our less than first class hotel, watching the other guests come and go. Our room, on an upper floor, was too small for the three of us to be comfortable; and it was high enough up that the view from the window showed us people looking like insects darting about their business. There was no television then, and my parents still had difficulty comprehending what they heard on the radio, although there were newscasts and programs like The Shadow and Jack Benny that would have been of interest had we been better able to understand them.

I was later to become thoroughly addicted to the afternoon adventure serials that were aimed at children—Jack Armstrong, Captain Midnight, Terry and The Pirates and, more than any of the others, Shafter Parker and His Circus. I think one of the reasons I tried very hard in school was so that I would never be detained, causing me to miss one of my beloved programs. These were to become my first escape from a confusing and daunting world I had come to not like very much.

While we were sitting in relatively comfortable wicker arm chairs in the hotel lobby my attention was drawn to a row of machines of a type I had never seen before, not even at my newly discovered miracle, the Automat. These wood and glass enclosed mechanical creatures seemed to be, when someone was attending to them, alive with lights and sounds and little metal balls that appeared to be the catalyst that touched off all the action.

Pinball machines were completely new to me. Unfortunately, not very many people were playing them and for the most part the machines stood idle and silent. When an occasional individual played, I watched in utter fascination.

I asked if I could go over to the machines to be able to observe them a little better.

My mother refused me the permission, but my father said there would be no harm in it.

I noticed that it was the metal plunger that caused the little balls to begin their travels, but when I pulled on one of them nothing happened. I tried again and again, but no ball emerged, nothing lit up and no sounds came from the machine. I failed to understand what I might be doing wrong.

The big man to my right was having no such problem. I watched him more carefully and became aware that periodically he was inserting a coin into a slot beside the plunger.

"You have to put a nickel in," he said, grinning at me. "Do you have any nickels?"

My innate shyness caused me to freeze. Besides, I had been admonished frequently never to speak with a strange man. Finally I shook my head and skipped back to where my parents were sitting.

"You have to put a nickel in," I said to them, translating into German exactly what the man had told me. "Can I have a nickel?"

"No," my mother replied. "We don't have money for games."

I wanted to play the machine so badly that my eyes filled with tears. "If I don't eat breakfast, can I have a nickel to play?" I asked.

"Don't be dumb," said my mother.

I didn't think I was being dumb. I was willing to make the trade-off. I was angry that I had no recourse and started to feel one of my temper tantrums coming on. On the other hand, I did not wish to make a scene in the hotel lobby, so I walked back to the machines.

This time I read the metal placard that was screwed to the front of each of the machines. I did not know some of the words, but I thought I understood what was meant. The signs said something like, "No minors allowed to play." Now, *that* I thought was dumb. I wondered whether it was because miners would have coal on their hands and would get the machines dirty. Surely miners were all old enough to know that they should wash before coming to the lobby to play the machines. It was beyond my slightly less than nine year old comprehension.

The big man was still working with the other pinball machine. He was bent over the top of it, alternately pulling on the plunger, tapping the side of the machine with one or both of his huge hands and snapping his fingers as if encouraging the little silver balls to strike more pay dirt. There were some immense numbers lit up across the upright screen, and lights flashed with unabating frenzy as the figures kept increasing.

Suddenly the last of the balls disappeared, and the man, in apparent anger, said a short word that I did not recognize, but I instinctively knew that it must be a bad word. He slapped the machine one last time but with much more force than previously and turned away.

I gingerly tried the plunger on the machine in front of me just in case it might possibly go into action, but nothing happened.

The man who had been playing the other machine saw my attempt. He came over to me, put his hand into the pocket of his jeans and pulled out a nickel.

"Here, kid," he said with a smile. "Give it a shot."

I did not comprehend his words, but there was no mistaking his offer of the five cent piece. My lifelong training in not accepting anything from strangers was almost forgotten, and I started to reach for the coin. Then I remembered and backed off.

The man's smile broadened, and he reached over to put the nickel into the slot. "There you go," he said.

I looked at the machine, watching the various numbers light up and then defer to the next in line. I was mesmerized.

"Go ahead," urged my benefactor. "Play it."

Rather tentatively I pulled the plunger and allowed it to strike the first silver ball. The sphere rolled slowly forward but did not get beyond the straight part of the chute before it rolled backward to its original resting place.

"You've got to pull back harder," the man said.

I tried again, and this time the ball took off. It bounced back and forth a few times rather lethargically, hit a bumper that lit up, rolled toward another one but failed to make sufficient contact to score, then glided back toward me and dropped from view.

"That's better. Do it still harder," I was admonished. The man reached down to put his hand over mine.

At that point my father got up from his chair and came over to the pinball area. He put his hand on my shoulder.

"This is my child," he said to the man, not unpleasantly, but with a firmness of purpose that could not be missed.

I fervently wished he had not interfered.

My new friend extended his hand to my father. "I know," he said, grinning. "I just thought she really wanted to try this machine."

My father hesitated briefly, then grasped the proffered hand. "Thank you, sir," he said in his thick accent. "I think she should not."

The man continued to grin. "It ain't going to hurt her," he said. "I know kids ain't supposed to play the machines, but who the hell is going to care about one nickel's worth? Besides, we're grownups here with her."

I do not believe that my father understood the entire speech, but at least his eyes smiled a little and there was a flicker at the corners of his lips. "You have to excuse my bad English," he said. "I only come to America yesterday."

With my father watching, the man helped me to play the remainder of the balls. The score was not very high. Then he joined us where we had been sitting and talked with us for a little while. The language barrier made the conversation difficult, but he managed to tell us that he was a truck driver and was awaiting a fresh load of something that he would deliver to a destination of which we had never heard. I did not grasp exactly what it was the man did, and undoubtedly neither did my parents; but it was our first personal contact with a real American. For that reason the fact remained with me that he was a truck driver—and that he had been very nice to me. I learned something very important from him—that one should never judge a person by whatever honest work he or she does for a living.

CHAPTER SIX

PLAYING HORSE

I DO NOT REMEMBER too much about my first few days of school in the United States. Even my memories of the first years are sketchy and incomplete. I do know that I felt very much a misfit, and a great deal about my school days was quite painful. Maybe that's why my recollections are not completely clear. I may have tried to block them out. I really wanted to love my new country and everything about it, but this simply was not possible.

To begin with, although my knowledge of the English language had increased exponentially during the year we had spent in England, I still had considerable difficulty with it. This was particularly the case with oral usage, when there was not much opportunity to think ahead about what needed to be spoken. From the beginning my reading comprehension was very good, and I did exceedingly well when required to write something, since I had time to think about it first. However, my accent was still very thick, and I had little knowledge of the popular American idiom. My classmates laughed at me whenever I spoke, and I became increasingly reluctant to do so.

The absolutely worst times of the school day for me were recess and lunch hour. I not only spoke strangely, as far as the other children were concerned, but I wore odd looking clothes, which my parents could not afford to replace with the styles that were being worn by other children. I also knew very little about the games that were played in American schoolyards and absolutely nothing regarding the traditions of United States holidays.

I have never been particularly athletic or graceful and have always lacked in coordination, so even mainly physical games with few rules, like jumping rope and keep-away, were very difficult for me. I tried very hard at first, but lacking encouragement and dreading the ridicule that invariably followed my miserable efforts, I soon began to avoid even casual contact with my classmates beyond what was absolutely required.

When the United States entered World War II in December of 1941 I was a little over ten years old, and interaction with my peers deteriorated even further at that time. As far as the other children were concerned, I was a German; and Germans were the enemy. I probably had very little understanding myself of the difference between being a German and being a Jewish refugee from Germany, so it was not possible for me to explain my status to my peers even if any of them were inclined to listen, which they weren't. My parents had informed me that the Nazi government had declared officially that all Jews were no longer German citizens. I tried to pass this information on to the other children, but it was a concept beyond their comprehension. I was from Germany, I spoke German, and I wore skirts and dresses that were different looking from theirs because these, too, came from Germany. Of course, to them that meant I was responsible for their fathers and older brothers having to go into the army and eventually off to war. The concept of "PC" had not yet been established, and youngsters in the 1940's were far less sophisticated than those who grew up post World War II. A few girls seemed to try to understand my situation, and I clung desperately to them. I tried to teach them some of the games I had started to play before being expelled from school in Germany, but they showed little interest in learning how to play them with me. I attempted to explain the very German craft of Scherenschnitte, the complex folding of a piece of paper and then cutting, with sharp scissors, various shapes into the multiple layers and then opening the paper out into an intricate lace doily. It was one of the few things I had learned that I felt might make an impression and, thus, a difference; but the girls were not at all impressed and for the most part not even interested. From among my meager possessions I brought to school a box full of little toys and trinkets with which I felt I could part and handed them out as tokens of friendship. The girls accepted the gifts with blank or quizzical stares, and then walked away. Some of them laughed. I definitely felt that I did not belong.

The school authorities had their own problems with me or with what to do with me. I had missed quite a bit of school, and then I had received some considerably accelerated education while in London. My limited skills with the English language made testing, as it was done in the early forties, extremely difficult. I was placed first in the high second grade, where I was older than the other children, and then, for a few days each, in the low third and high third. I finally came to rest in the low fourth grade, where I quickly caught up and began to do very well academically. Socially I remained rather hopelessly an outcast.

Among the few who accepted me in spite of my difference were two very volatile sisters of definitely Irish Catholic extraction, June and Benardine Shanahan. Benardine was nearly the same age as I, and June was a year or so older. It turned out that they lived in a flat almost across the street from my apartment house. Benardine and I were alternately the best of friends and worlds apart. She delighted in teasing me when I made a mistake in pronunciation or committed some other minor gaffe. June often told her to be quiet, but when Benardine was on one of her unpredictable tangents, she could not be silenced. June herself often lectured me on my mistakes. From the two of them I received a considerable amount of information and education about the Catholic religion, which their family followed devoutly. They often told me that I was a heathen, since I now knew what was the true religion and still did not wish to convert. I did not completely understand what they were talking about until years later. On the other hand, I didn't much care either. This religious aspect to my relationship with the Shanahan girls became one of the many things I did not discuss with my parents for fear of being blamed for yet another problem that kept me from making friends.

The three of us nearly always walked home together and sometimes even walked to school together in the mornings. I probably owe much of my eventual almost complete Americanization to June and Benardine Shanahan. That conversion included some use of inappropriate language for a ten or eleven year old.

Our friendship was not destined to last very long. Less than a year after I had met the two sisters, the small neighborhood elementary school we had been attending was closed. The students were transferred to Raphael Weill Elementary School, a much larger facility that was not only quite a few blocks further away but was located in a predominantly ethnic part of town. The children there were mostly black, Filipino or Asian. The Shanahans refused to let their two girls go there and enrolled them instead in a private Catholic school, where, naturally, they met a new set of best friends. I still saw them occasionally, but within a short time the Shanahan family moved to Petaluma, north of the San Francisco Bay Area, to operate a chicken farm and I never saw them again after that.

I was devastated. Again I was alone and facing the same lonely difficulties I had encountered when first starting school in the United States.

One of the transfers to Raphael Weill was a tall sixth grader who seemed much too mature for elementary school. Her name was Joyce, and she had flaming, flowing red hair that glowed in the sun. I admired and probably envied that glorious hair, but what interested me most about Joyce was that she had a single passion in life. That passion was for horses. Raised on a ranch and then forced to move to the city with her divorced mother, Joyce spent her recess time playing horse with anyone who was willing. She was always the rider or driver, using the other girl's belt or loose folds of blouse or skirt as reins. Each recess they would gallop around the yard in tandem until the bell rang. When bad weather forced us to remain inside, Joyce always read books about horses or horsemanship or she drew pictures—always of horses. She was, I recall, quite talented at drawing. Sometimes she also drew pictures of horses while in the classroom and would be sent to the principal's office. Two or three times the principal even suspended her for her lack of attention.

I had noticed Joyce almost immediately and became keenly aware of her ability for drawing horses. I admired her talent, but I admired her even more for her singular devotion to these animals. Not that I was particularly a horse lover myself, but I had begun to feel that animals—all animals—could be much better friends than people had shown themselves to be. Much of my own free reading time was spent reading about animals.

Three or four times I approached Joyce either to admire her

drawings or to see what she was reading. She was never without at least one book about horses under her arm, and usually she carried several. Some of these were her own and some were from the public library. It was from Joyce that I learned about the library and the wonders I might find there. Until then I had thought that the library contained only storybooks of the kind teachers required fourth graders to read. Most of those did not interest me.

I secretly wished that Joyce would pay more attention to me. I would have liked to know her better, perhaps to have her as a best friend. I often hoped that she would invite me to play horse with her, but the bid never came. Nevertheless, by telling me about the library she had given me something of very great value.

I began to visit the library on Saturdays. We lived about seven city blocks away, and it was an easy walk even for a child—especially one whose family did not own a car. Walking was very important in our lives.

I became an avid reader, nearly always choosing books about animals, both fiction and reference. I read about domestic pets and about the wildlife of the tropics and other distant parts of the world. In the next few years I managed to check out every volume the library had about dogs. I discovered Albert Payson Terhune and zealously absorbed all of his writings. Without ever having owned a dog I became a fervent dog lover, and I began to feel very strongly that I would be much happier if there could be a dog in my life.

Of course dogs were not allowed in our apartment building, and no amount of pleading and cajoling had any effect. I promised that if I were allowed to keep a dog I would train it to be quiet, and the landlord would never know about it. I threatened to run away with my dog if I could not keep him at home. I also threatened to run away if I could not have a dog. My parents did not take this forewarning in the least seriously beyond my mother apprising me that such talk would result in severe punishment if I repeated it. I became completely obsessed with wanting a dog. I also began to write short stories, most of them fantasies revolving around dogs or around other childhood desires that most likely could never come true for me.

In the early forties, before the Cow Palace was built, the Golden Gate Kennel Club used to put on an all-breed dog show once a year in the San Francisco Civic Auditorium, which was not far from the library and, therefore, not far from where we lived. The show ran for two days—Saturday and Sunday. As soon as I saw posters advertising the event I begged money for the admission fee from my father. He was always much more likely than my mother to understand such a request, and he gave me enough to get into the show and, knowing that I would spend the entire day there, to buy some food. Each year I could scarcely contain my excitement as I waited for the big weekend to arrive.

I rose early and was at the Civic Auditorium on Saturday morning before the doors opened. I had sneaked into the kitchen while my parents were still in bed and made myself a bologna sandwich, which I shoved into a pocket of my jacket. I knew that I would need money to purchase a ticket for Sunday, so I planned to save my lunch money for that purpose. I knew that even my father would not understand my need to attend the dog show on both days and would not give me money for Sunday's admission. Money, especially for any kind of entertainment, was still very scarce for us in those days.

For the next few years I did the same thing each January when the dog show came to town. On both days I would arrive first thing in the morning and would stay until the latest possible hour that would still get me home in time for dinner. I knew better than to stretch the patience of my parents when it came to not being at home at mealtime.

Once at the show I was in another world. I did not understand about the judging, so I did not watch too much of it; but I looked at every dog of every breed in the benching area. Sometimes I even had the courage to ask an owner who appeared congenial if I might pet the dog. If the owner seemed extremely approachable, I asked questions. I began to learn about the different breeds. I found out about catalogs and saw that they contained a virtual treasure trove of information. It became apparent to me that I could not successfully appreciate the show without one. They cost, I believe, a dollar then; but it might as well have been a hundred. After stewing about my lack of funds for several hours I did something that was for me unheard of. I spotted an unattended catalog lying on an empty chair, and, approaching stealthily, I appropriated it. Yes, I stole it. I felt extremely guilty, knowing all too well that what I had done was wrong; but the joy of having this great reference eventually helped to wipe out that feeling.

I spent quite a bit of time at the Collie benching, since I was fresh from reading several volumes of Terhune. One woman who had several Collies entered in the show went out of her way to be nice to me, and for several years I went back to talk with her whenever I went to a show. She was from Marin County and invited me to visit her kennel, but of course, sadly, I had no way to do that.

In those far more guileless days of the forties the Golden Gate Kennel Club used to give away several purebred puppies each day as door prizes to encourage the sale of more admission tickets. The puppies were kept in a pen near the entrance to the show, and I would spend much time squatting beside them and talking to them, picking my favorites and hoping against hope that I might win one. I thought that my parents might be sufficiently impressed by the value of one of these prizes that, should I be fortunate enough to win one, I would be allowed to keep it. I also foraged the nooks and crannies of the building and scavenged the trash bins for tickets that might have been dropped or discarded. Since the winners were required to be present at the time of the drawing, which was rather late in the afternoon, many stubs were junked by people who did not wish to stay. I usually wound up with two dozen or more numbers, and I always anxiously awaited the prize drawing; but I never won, which, now that I look back on it, was probably a good thing.

Although my love affair with dogs and dog shows received a very early start, it would be more than twenty years before my dream of actually having a canine of my own came true. Perhaps that is why I overreacted and ultimately wound up with a houseful of them.

CHAPTER SEVEN

ADOLESCENCE

From what I have written thus far it is probably apparent that I had a very difficult childhood. My adolescence was even worse. I suppose that the peculiar and alienating lessons learned as a lonely little girl did much to prepare me for failure in the often traumatic school of puberty.

I read incessantly. Books were my best friends. They were almost my *only* friends. For the most part I read books about animals and the fascinating relationships some people had with them. Oddly enough, I also became fascinated with action comic books, which fueled my hormone kindled imagination. I not only read avidly about the various caped crusaders but when deprived of reading material or opportunity for any length of time, in my mind's eye I would soar off to rescue the underdog, visualizing myself transformed into a super heroine possessed of incredible supernatural powers. I wove together fanciful and intricate scenarios in which my interest in all phases of science resulted in a potion that could turn my uncoordinated body into a precision instrument of muscle and incredible abilities. Sometimes I could fly, and in my daydreams I would propel myself through blue and cloudless skies on missions of mercy to the far and often exotic corners of the world. Later, as I proceeded into my teens, these fantasies changed somewhat, and I would become the maiden in distress who was rescued from a terrible fate by a handsome masked and caped superhero. Eventually, as I underwent pubescence, these imaginary adventures began to bear some sexual undertones, which I did not in the least understand. I knew better than to ask my mother.

There were also some flights into fantasies of violence, as re-reading my diaries from middle school and high school have revealed. I find a few of the things I wrote in those volumes of emotional outpourings hard to believe and even more difficult to accept the fact that I had written them. The ink on some of the pages is smeared, and I have no doubt that the source of the stains was bitter tears. Some of these writings have given me an all too clear understanding of what occurred at Columbine and several other schools in recent years.

Attending movies, especially in the second run theaters, was incredibly cheap in the forties. Fifteen cents would admit a youngster to a nearly endless world of magic created by the running of two feature films repeatedly. During school vacations my mother would give me fifteen cents as she left for work in the morning so that the movies could serve as my baby sitter, much in the way television is often used by today's parents. I was a latchkey kid almost from the day we had arrived in San Francisco and my mother started seeking some kind of work, settling into one dreary, ill-paying job after another. Setting off on foot for Market Street at ten o'clock in the morning would bring me to that then wondrous street of many motion picture houses by the time they opened. Frequently I would sit through both movies twice. It was better than being at home alone. The optical overload may have had something to do with the poor distance vision that has plagued me since the age of ten or eleven and continues to this day.

As the troubled years of my adolescence began, although my imagination still took me to places I would never see, I had enough intelligence to realize that my less than ravishing physiognomy and introverted nature would preclude my ever having a string of dashingly handsome heroes on hand. It was likely that there wouldn't be even one. More than ever, books, the movies and animals made up my world—at least the one in which I wanted to live.

By the time I reached the age of twelve the reality of never owning a dog while we occupied our Franklin Street apartment had sunk in. The thought remained in the back of my mind, but by then I had discovered an alternate source of enchantment and satisfaction—the zoo. In the forties and fifties admission to

Fleischacker Zoo was, fortunately, still free. My father had taken me there two or three times on Sundays, and on my first visit I had decided that I would be a zoo director when I grew up. The thought of being responsible for and loved by all those fascinating creatures set off a spark within me that might have propelled me into a course of action that could have guided my destiny to something really meaningful, had I received any kind of encouragement.

Although our apartment and the zoo were at nearly diagonally opposite ends of the city, it did not take me long to find a way to get to the zoo on my own. During my summer vacation my mother still gave me fifteen cents before she left for work in the morning, fifteen cents that would get me into the movie of my choice, providing I would walk both to and from the theater. Ten cents would also buy a streetcar ride to the zoo and leave me enough change to purchase a small bag of peanuts or popcorn that I could feed to the animals. I am not sure of the actual distance in miles that I had to walk home, but even at a brisk pace the jaunt took about two and a half hours. It was probably about eight miles. My mother arrived at home from work at quarter to six, give or take a few minutes; and I knew that I had to be there by then. That meant I had to leave the zoo by three o'clock. I did not want to tell my mother where I had been. She had already begun to belittle and to ridicule my obsession with animals, and I had no desire to attempt to argue my case. There was no chance that I could ever win, and there was a strong likelihood that if she knew what I was doing with it I would no longer receive the daily stipend.

I spent two summer vacations going to the zoo almost every weekday. The ride by bus and streetcar took about forty minutes, and I would leave the house as soon after my mother had left as I could get bathed and dressed and make myself a sandwich to take along. Since there was no admission fee, there were no gates. It was possible to walk into the zoo at any hour, and early morning held its own lure. Cages were being cleaned. Animals were being fed. Keepers were busy with their morning chores. All of it attracted me like some many-tentacled magnetic octopus.

I expended hours watching certain animals that particularly appealed to me, such as Puddles, the hippopotamus. I never tired of watching Puddles' keeper toss apples into the animal's gaping mouth. Eventually the keeper began to recognize me, and sometimes he would allow me to throw an apple or two. I found Puddles' ungainliness as he plodded down his concrete steps into the water to exude a kind of negative grace. I can still see him submerging himself, only nostrils, eyes and ears remaining in view, looking like bumpy parts of a shiny, brown log. I still chuckle at the memory of the wild, gyroscopic motion of that silly screw tail, a ritual that invariably preceded or accompanied Puddles' act of relieving himself. I would wait a long time in order to see this. It was worth the wait.

I never missed the two daily performances of the sea lion show, and I knew at what time the apes and the caged monkeys were usually fed. The simians that roamed free on Monkey Island were another favorite attraction. I tried to spend my last half hour or so each day at Monkey Island, because there were several benches and I could sit for a while before undertaking the long trek home.

It bothered me that I was forced to spend so much of my time walking. It was time that I could be spending with my beloved animals. Instead, it was necessary for me to leave in mid-afternoon to begin my homeward journey. It was not the walk itself that annoyed me but the boring repetitiousness of it. No matter how I tried to vary my route, it was always the same dreary two and a half hour hike. There were several ways to go that would have afforded some lovely city views, but they entailed a considerable amount of uphill climbing.

That would lengthen the time it took to return home; so most of the time I followed one of the more level and therefore quicker routes.

At the end of summer I missed my zoo visits very much and tried to make up for the loss by reading more animal books. When I brought these home from the library I told my mother that they were an assignment from school. Of course she told me that I should be starting to read romances and books on how to make myself more attractive rather than the kind of literature that was occupying so much of my time.

The summer I turned thirteen there was a job opening with a local manufacturer of advertising specialties. The company had requested three students to help with a short term project. I was very shy and hesitant about applying, having never worked before nor gone through the process of applying for a job. My parents insisted strongly that I should go.

Two classmates and I went to see the owner of the firm, and he promptly hired the three of us. The pay was below minimum wage and the work was, I realized some time later, far too hazardous for young teenagers to do. Our employer had bought a huge batch of old five by seven inch and eight by ten inch glass photographic plates for very little money. He planned to use them as the glass part of framed calendars. In the forties, before the arrival of plastic novelties, these were popular as an advertising specialty. To use the plates they first had to be soaked in containers of lye to soften the photographic emulsion. Then the emulsion had to be carefully removed with a scrubber. The plates were then given a final rinse and set in racks to dry. If these steps were properly carried out, the plates could be used as picture frame glass. They were exactly the right size and of the proper thickness and were quite a bit cheaper than new glass that would have to be cut to order.

For this process to be cost effective it had to be done very rapidly and with the cheapest possible labor. That was why the three of us were hired. We were to soak and clean thousands of these plates and then to help the regular employees in assembling the calendars.

The plates first had to be checked over so that cracked or badly chipped ones could be eliminated. Then the good ones had to be loaded onto metal racks, which were lowered into the lye. Since the full racks were quite heavy this part of the operation fell to the only boy in our threesome, a cheerful troublemaker by the name of Harry Hoffman. Harry and I had attended a movie and a studio broadcast together during the preceding term, which, I suppose, could be constituted in those days as dating; but I remember him most vividly for an incident in school that I have never forgotten and have always considered to be a masterpiece in tailoring punishment to fit the crime.

Our seventh grade English class was held in one of those supposedly temporary buildings hurriedly added to bulging schools in areas that had a huge influx of defense workers and their families during World War II. The wooden structure was just large enough to house a single classroom, with a dividing wall behind the teacher's desk partitioning off the cloakroom. A string of these rapidly erected cottages ringed the school's playground and exercise yard. The buildings were poorly constructed, with unfinished open beam ceilings and little or no insulation. One day while our teacher was reading some poetry aloud, Harry sneaked into the cloakroom and entertained the class by chinning himself on the beams. His performance went on for several minutes before someone in the class giggled, causing the teacher to look up from his book. Noting that the eyes of most of the class were focused on the entrance to the cloakroom, he turned quickly and caught Harry in the act.

"Mr. Hoffman, you are very athletic," he said quickly. "Perhaps you would like to continue your exercise program outside."

He then ordered Harry to run several laps around the yard while allowing the amused students to stand at the windows to watch. I had always admired this particular teacher, and I thought his handling of Harry's clowning was nothing short of sublime. Unfortunately, the incident very nearly resulted in the teacher's suspension when Harry's parents complained about cruel and unusual punishment.

For his part of the job that summer when we worked together Harry was given a rubber apron and thick gloves and a warning not to allow the lye to splash on anything. The other girl, Dorothy Shumate, and I did the scrubbing. We were shown briefly how to do it and how to stack the cleaned plates for drying, but nothing was said about the dangerously sharp edges on the glass. Considering the nearly constant prodding to work faster, it was a miracle that none of us incurred any serious injury. In spite of the apron and gloves, Harry suffered a few minor burns and ruined a pair of shoes and several pairs of corduroy trousers, while Dorothy and I learned to live without complaining too much about our constantly cut or nicked hands.

There was some educational benefit to this near slave labor. For instance, the three of us developed a viable code language in which we were able to converse freely even while our hated boss was within earshot. By substituting words that seemed completely irrelevant to their context we enjoyed the satisfaction of berating him under his very nose. The only actual term I still remember is that we used, for whatever obscure reason that escaped me long ago, the words "the truth" to mean, "Watch it, the boss is coming!"

It also felt very adult and pleasingly vulgar to be able to call this parsimonious opportunist, via a privately cryptic synonym, absolutely the strongest epithet known to me at that time—a shitass.

Our other source of amusement was the telephone. The company number was the same but for a single digit as the number of the county hospital, and calls came frequently from distraught friends and relatives of patients. When our employer was away we were expected to answer the phone and take messages. It was probably Harry who first informed one of these wrong number callers that he had reached not the hospital but the city morgue.

I had enough of this odious job after two or three days and wanted desperately to give it up, but, as I might have expected, my parents were convinced that I was exaggerating when I told them of the conditions under which we were required to labor. They would not hear of my quitting. Harry and Dorothy needed the money even more than I did. We were all too young and inexperienced to have much chance of getting other employment for the summer; so we continued until our last week of vacation, counting the days until we would be emancipated. On our first day of freedom the three of us went to the now defunct amusement park, Playland at the Beach, and rode several of the rides, a fun-filled outing none of us had ever been able to afford before. The following day I took most of my remaining money and bought a huge stack of animal books. It was the beginning of my first such collection.

In my first year of high school I had a serious crush on a tall, handsome and very stupid basketball player who had failed several classes and was repeating sophomore English. I watched him quite a bit from a safe distance and created elaborate fantasies in my mind about him. He was probably completely unaware of my existence until one day as we were leaving class he asked me to help him with some grammar exercises in our textbook that he did not understand. I explained the lesson to him, and he smiled his engaging smile at me when he thanked me. It was the only time he ever spoke to me. My heart raced and I was tongue-tied for the remainder of the day.

More enduring and infinitely more serious was my infatuation with a fellow student in my art class. I was a sophomore and he was a senior. Stanley was a quiet, serious young man with a sturdy physique, almost swarthy complexion and classic Jewish features. The way I remember him, he slightly resembled Robert Alda, a movie actor who was quite popular in the 1940's. I considered him handsome, but what probably attracted me to him was his extreme maturity in both appearance and demeanor compared to most of the loud and giddy high schoolers who ignored me and whom I had quickly grown to dislike.

Stanley, unlike most of the others in the class, had some real talent for drawing. Nearly everyone who chose freehand drawing as an elective did so to get an easy credit instead of taking another "solid" course that would involve heavy studying and yet more weighty homework assignments. I had chosen it partly for that reason—it was very difficult for me to concentrate on homework in our small apartment once my parents were at home—and partly in hope that I might discover that I had some talent for art. I don't.

I felt strongly attracted to Stanley almost from the first day of school and probably spent more time watching him than I did on my own project. Timid as I was, I managed to ask him frequently for help and suggestions. He was always kind and quietly amiable but never volunteered any information about himself. Of course I fantasized about him. For much of the term he was my Prince Charming, and I continued to do everything possible to make sure that I would be positioned next to him whenever we were sketching. I rarely saw him except during art class, although I tried very hard to learn more about him, his other classes and what else he did.

I knew that Stanley was a high senior and that he would be leaving George Washington High School at the end of the term, probably to be out of my life forever unless I could do something to attract him. That possibility, I was aware, was not very strong. I was not only a lowly sophomore and probably three years or more his junior, but I was a shy, unpopular, bespectacled, plain Jane with serious difficulties in relating to my peers—especially the male ones.

One day I asked Stanley what he was going to do after graduation, and he told me that he planned to attend business school. The details have grown dim over the years, but he talked very freely to me about his plans and then about himself. I did not completely realize it then, but he was a bit of a maverick. In spite of his seriousness, he was not a very good student and completing high school had not come easily to him. He was nearly nineteen, which suggested that he had probably even failed a grade or two. He was a quiet loner by choice and spent most of his free time pursuing a dedicated involvement with the sport of archery.

As soon as Stanley had told me about his love of archery I had immediate and vividly detailed visions of him dressed as Robinhood, patrolling Sherwood Forest with longbow at the ready. He looked wonderful in his green tights.

I knew that archery was not a sport offered by George Washington High School, so I asked him where he practiced. He told me about the archery range in Golden Gate Park.

"Do you go there often?" I asked.

"Every day after school and most weekends," he replied. His face seemed to light up when he talked about his passion.

After that I spoke with Stanley whenever possible before and during class, a ploy that did not go unnoticed by some other students, including Harry Hoffman. Harry and one or two others began to tease me a little about having a "thing" for Stanley. I was horribly embarrassed and lived in mortal fear that it would get back to the object of my adoration. It did not stop me from daydreaming about Stanley, and I suppose that in my immaturity and lack of experience I was not very subtle about my feelings for him.

One day about two weeks before graduation Stanley asked me if I had ever tried a bow and arrows. I admitted that I hadn't.

"Would you like to go with me?" he asked. "I can teach you how to shoot."

I was as if thunderstruck, ecstatic and simultaneously wondering whether I had heard him correctly. It was a moment frozen in time, and then I realized that he was gently smiling at me, awaiting my reply.

"I'd like that," I said. "Very much."

Stanley said he would pick me up on Saturday at nine. We could go to the archery range for a few hours and then maybe have lunch.

Our date went well. Stanley was not a big talker, but he was easy to be with even for a socially awkward and introverted teenager like me. Of course I was clumsier than ever when I attempted to follow his instructions for shooting the bow. I marveled at his prowess when he demonstrated proper form and could not take my eyes away from the broad back and shoulders and the rippling muscles under his snugly fitting polo shirt. I could have stood there watching him until the end of time.

The next school day the boys who had previously teased me about Stanley cornered me on the way to art class. How they had learned about the archery outing I have no idea, but they knew and they renewed their harassing with great enthusiasm. My discomfiture had me nearly in tears. I was afraid to talk with Stanley that day other than to tell him what a wonderful time I had had with him.

I never saw Stanley again after his graduation, and eventually the passage of time erased the hurt. I honestly believe that my Twentieth Century Robinhood's invitation had been a genuine act of charity as well as chivalry, and, in retrospect, I still love him for it.

Geburtsurkunde

(Standesamt Stuttgart Nr. 3505/1931).

Lilian Bauer –

ist am 2. August 1931 – – – – – – – – – – – – – – – – – – –

in Stuttgart geboren.

Vater: Siegfried Bauer, Kaufmann, wohnhaft in Stuttgart.

Mutter: Gertrude Auguste geborene Horkheimer, wohnhaft wie oben, – – – – – – – – – – – – – – – –

Änderungen der Eintragung: Die Obengenannte hat den weiteren Vornamen Sara angenommen. – – – – – – – – – – – – –

Stuttgart, den 2. Januar 1939.

Der Standesbeamte

In Vertretung: *Kegel*

(Siegel)

This is the official document ("Birth Transfer Agreement") sent by the German government in January of 1939 to declare that I had assumed the additional name of Sara. To all practical purposes, this was a new birth certificate that indicated to whoever saw it that I was a Jew. My parents each received one that added the name Sara to my mother's name and Israel to my father's.

CHAPTER EIGHT

ALEX

I ALWAYS HAD THE feeling that I was supposed to be impressed with my Uncle Alex. However, not only was he not my uncle, but even at the age of nine I was not at all taken with him. Well, actually I *was* impressed by the fact that he owned a new car—an ugly, dung colored 1940 Packard. He was the first relative I had ever met or even known about who owned a car at all except the mysterious Toni in London, and she didn't really seem to be a relative. At the time Alex came to meet us at the train station in Oakland when we first arrived in the Bay Area I had no idea that nearly everyone in the United States owned a car. For a very brief moment in time I thought Alex must be very special.

Alex Bauer was middle aged and probably one of the homeliest men I had ever seen. He was the son of Simon Bauer, the distant cousin of my father's who had signed the affidavit and put up the necessary guarantee to enable us to come to the United States as immigrants. Simon had been quite ill at the time he had endorsed the papers to show that the Bauer refugee family from Germany would not become a public liability. By the time our quota number had been called and we were able to leave England for America, Simon had passed away.

It was fortunate for us that Simon had lived as long as he did, for Alex, undoubtedly, would never have accepted such a responsibility. Alex was a crude, uneducated man who had never learned how to love.

If he had not been so obese and slovenly, Alex might not have been quite so unpleasant looking. He was a big man, tall and broad shouldered. He had inherited the gene for early and complete baldness, a curse with which nearly all the Bauer men have lived. His face was round and jowly and usually unshaven, although the complexion under the stubble was ruddy and tanned, except what was always shaded by his ever present, sweat stained hat. His eyes were a deep blue that could blaze with anger at the slightest provocation. His lips were thick and slack and were usually wrapped around the disgusting remnant of a fat cigar. Whenever the necessity of eating forced him to remove the stogie, flecks of soggy tobacco remained on his lips.

In the ten years that followed our arrival in San Francisco I became all too familiar with that face. Alex was a perennial dinner guest in our apartment, and his normal place at the table was across from me, where it was quite difficult to avoid being privy to his piggish appearance and table manners.

Alex and his brother, Samuel, had inherited the Bauer Cooperage Company, a grimy and prosaic but highly profitable business that dealt in the purchase, reconditioning and resale of used wooden barrels and metal storage drums. Both boys had been plucked from school and put to work in the family enterprise at an early age. Simon Bauer, whom I never knew, evidently had no regard at all for the value of learning and education. Both of his sons could barely read or write.

Alex and Samuel had worked hard, long hours from early childhood and had never had the opportunity to enjoy the fruits of their labor. Samuel had married quite young and was apparently a devoted family man with a fair-haired, attractive daughter, Juliana. His wife, perhaps to counteract the lack of culture of her husband, had seen to it that Juliana had all the advantages of an upper middle class family. She was sent to dancing lessons, piano lessons, singing lessons, acting lessons and to charm school. At some point along the line her mother decided that Juliana had the beauty and talent necessary to become a movie star. The two of them made several trips to Hollywood. Juliana and I attended the same high school, and she frequently appeared on the program at a rally or assembly; but I have no idea whatever became of her or her stage mother's dream. Juliana and I were worlds apart during our high school years and barely knew one another beyond a perfunctory "Hello" when we encountered one another somewhere in the school's hallways or staircases.

Alex, on the other hand, did not take the time as a young man to find an appropriate mate. His only recreation had been baseball, and when we met him it still was. He held season tickets and always attended as many games as he could. San Francisco at that time boasted only a minor league team, the Seals, but Alex was a great fan. As a youngster he had played as much sandlot ball as his severe work schedule would allow, and he still participated in an occasional softball game. He knew all the ins and outs of baseball and could recite the pitching and batting records of all the past and current greats. At first he attempted to impart his fondness for baseball on my father. I do not believe that my father had ever had any interest in spectator team sports—even the European ones like soccer; and he steadfastly turned down the invitations from Alex. Occasionally Alex took me to a game, which I eventually learned to enjoy; but spending the better part of a day with this revolting relative to attend a Sunday doubleheader was never a great pleasure.

Alex was twice married and twice divorced to and from the same incredibly tanned and artificially animated woman named Rita. Where he and Rita had met I have no idea, but they were a total mis-match. Rita's part of the marriage most likely consisted of accommodating his occasional sexual needs, while Alex supplied a comfortable apartment and sufficient pocket money to enable her to carry on the lifestyle to which she had aspired. Mostly that lifestyle consisted of spending her days on the beach, burning her body into a near African skin tone and toying with an endless string of professional wrestlers. Rita hardly ever accompanied Alex anywhere. For that matter, Alex rarely went anywhere other than to his work, to a baseball game or to our place for dinner. Rita was not Jewish, so she definitely did not go with Alex to synagogue on Rosh Hashanah and Yom Kippur, the only time he ever set foot inside the temple.

Alex was neither a generous man nor a charitable one, although by most standards he would be considered wealthy. He knew, however, how to make the most of whatever magnanimity he chose to display. For instance, once or twice a month he would go to one of the Jewish grocery stores that abounded on McAllister street, not far from where we lived, and fill two large paper bags with an eclectic mix of foods, mostly items he himself relished. He would then appear at our door and, of course, be invited to stay for a meal. This was, most of the time, on a weekend and in addition to his almost nightly dinner with us after driving my father home from the cooperage. The dinner invitations for Alex began almost immediately after we came to San Francisco. The day after we had moved into our apartment he turned up at our door with the first of the bags of groceries, leaving my mother no choice but to ask him to stay.

My father, who had never done any manual labor in his life, began work at the Bauer Cooperage within days after our arrival. Alex had deposited us in an apartment he had rented in our name in a three-story apartment house at the corner of Franklin and Turk Streets, just at the edge of what was then known as the tenderloin district. It was not a very good neighborhood, but the rent, at $40 per month, was cheap and the building was a reasonably clean and reputable one (there were seven apartments on each story, and I think the unofficial limit was one hooker per floor). The location was also within walking distance of shopping, schools, public transportation and even, if one was not adverse to longer walks, downtown and the then famous Market Street and its many department stores and other shopping opportunities. In 1940, San Francisco's downtown was still the vibrant heart of the city and offered everything a resident might need or want.

My father's job, at least the official part of it, was to load and unload trucks. It was dirty, physically demanding and stultifying work for an intellectually inclined man in his mid-fifties who had been accustomed to running his own business; but nothing in my father's past life had prepared him for any other way to support his wife and daughter in a new country, where he barely spoke the language. Besides, he had accepted the position at the time Simon Bauer had agreed to vouch for us; and my father, above all else, was a man of pride and honor—even if it would eventually kill him.

If anyone thought there would be special perks for my father because he was a relative, they were very wrong. My father was paid what any beginning cooper's helper received; and there were no fringe benefits. He rode a streetcar to work each day, nearly an hour's journey. In exchange for a ride home he spent an extra hour or more helping to clean up the office, for which he received no additional pay; and Alex nearly always stayed for dinner after bringing him home in the Packard.

Alex talked with his mouth full, dribbled food down the front of his vest—he always wore a shabby three-piece suit—and smacked his lips loudly as he ate. We made certain that he always used the same chair, since he would sit with his legs spread wide and allow bits of food to fall onto the upholstery between his knees. No matter where we placed an ashtray, his cigar butt always reposed on the edge of the table and permeated the air with its acrid stench.

There could be no conversation at dinner other than to listen to Alex and to nod in agreement. He complained incessantly about his employees, his customers, his wife (to whom he referred most of the time simply as "She" and at other times as "The Bitch"). Mostly he would rant and rave about Sam and "The Kid". The Kid was another cousin, a few years younger than Alex, who was the office manager at Bauer Cooperage. Alex was quite certain that both Sam and The Kid were embezzling from him. No one seemed to do enough work or to have enough intelligence to suit Alex. Nothing ever went smoothly enough to please him. His vocabulary was as limited as his education, and instead of varying it he would shout the same words and trite terms with increasing volume, usually accompanied by bits of food flying from his mouth. If he happened to be in an unusually good mood he would talk about baseball, but always the conversation would drift back to center on his own miserable existence.

Alex rarely gave gifts even on occasions like birthdays, Christmas or Chanukah; but when I was about to graduate from high school he surprised all of us by asking me what I wanted for graduation. I had never owned a wristwatch and had really hoped for one, so I told him. I did not believe he would come through with something so frivolous, but he did. I was amazed and very pleased.

The one thing for which Alex always paid was our seats at Temple Beth Israel for the High Holidays. I have never been able to figure out why it was so important for him to have the three of us attend services with him. He was neither religious nor given to showing off. I was not at all religious even then but I really enjoyed sitting behind two celebrities who attended services in that synagogue—Sophie Tucker and Metropolitan Opera star Jan Peerce.

The first divorce came as quite a surprise. Alex had known for some time that Rita was spending most of the days while he was at the cooperage entertaining her wrestler friends on the beach. He often had complained about it, but his attitude seemed no different from his impotent rage against employees he felt were stealing from him. It was as if he considered Rita's infidelity to be an inescapable fact of life. One day he simply told my father that he was throwing Rita out of their apartment and that he had already spoken to his attorney, an all-purpose legal agent by the name of Axelrod. Axelrod advised Alex not only in business matters but counseled him on his personal affairs whenever it was required as well. Alex complained about Axelrod too, accusing him of being a money grabber and a few other unsavory things, but Axelrod was probably as close to a friend as Alex ever had.

The separation lasted for less than six months, and I do not believe that the divorce was ever final. One day Alex seemed less gruff than usual—almost cheerful; and he informed us that Rita was coming home. He had been calling on her for some time at the small apartment into which she had moved and for which he evidently had been paying.

For a time things were all sweetness and light between Alex and Rita. Or at least it looked that way. They even invited us to their apartment one Saturday for dinner. I don't remember much about the occasion except that it looked as if Rita had gone to some trouble. There were candles in silver holders on the table, and the food was very good. My mother and father had sometimes discussed the fact that Rita apparently knew neither how to keep house nor how to cook. She and Alex had most likely hired someone for the day to clean up the apartment and to prepare the meal.

The second time Alex divorced Rita was less than amicable. She wanted, and received, quite a bit of money, and the final settlement also included having the rent paid permanently on the Marina apartment, in which she continued to live. Alex had hired a private detective to obtain proof of Rita's infidelity, which I am certain was not difficult to do. After all, everyone including myself knew about Rita and her wrestlers; but for some reason he gave in to most of her demands. When he moved out of their flat he accepted an invitation from The Kid to live with his family until he could get himself squared away. He stayed for over a year, while The Kid felt that he was assuring himself of a substantial inheritance by allowing Alex to remain as a non-paying and undoubtedly difficult boarder. For the first time ever I was glad we lived in such a small apartment, one that was not large enough to even consider inviting Alex to stay with us.

By that time my father had retired. In his sixties, he could no longer perform the heavy work demanded of him, although for several years Alex had been allowing him to spend a few hours each day in the office rather than on the loading dock.

Surprisingly enough to everyone, Alex met and married Charlotte, a woman quite a few years his junior. She was a very well bred, educated and cultured Jewish lady who managed to bring some modicum of refinement into his life. She induced him to buy a house, a large, beautifully appointed residence in the Park-Presidio district. She made it for Alex into the first real home he had ever known. She showed him the pleasures of travel and attempted to teach him how to live gracefully and graciously. They went to Mexico, to Hawaii and to the Caribbean, always traveling in first class luxury.

Alex lived another five or six years and left almost his entire estate, which was of considerable size, to his widow. He bequeathed to my father, who by then was in a nursing home and very ill with Parkinson's disease and what would now be diagnosed as Alzheimer's, a thousand dollars. No one else received as much as a dime. The Kid, Sam and other family members fought bitterly over the inheritance, but I firmly believe that Charlotte had earned every cent she received. I think the few years of their marriage represented the only time in his life that Alex had known any real happiness. Charlotte may have married him for his money, but she had worked diligently at fulfilling her obligations as a wife to him. I begrudge her absolutely nothing.

⋐⋑

CHAPTER NINE

RADIO DAYS

There were two things that were ultra important to me during our first few years in the United States. One of them was the public library and the other, in those pre-television days, was the radio. I spent much time absorbing material from both of these sources, and I credit the latter for at least part of my ability to speak English without an accent.

Fortunately we lived close enough to the main branch of the San Francisco public library that I could easily walk there and back. I made the trip every Saturday, spending hours in the reference room, pouring over books that could not be taken out. When I knew that it would soon be time for me to leave, I would load up with as many volumes that could be checked out as my library card allowed and would take them home.

Then there was the radio. As I mentioned in a previous chapter, I became not merely devoted but thoroughly addicted to the daily episodes of the various radio serials aimed at children and teens that were popular in the far more naive forties. I would sit with my ear glued to our old, dome topped radio that someone—I am not certain who—had given us after learning that we did not have a radio. I did not want to miss a single word of the stories; and, of course, with no guidance that things might be otherwise, I believed every inflated promise made by the commercials. Most of the sponsors were manufacturers of breakfast cereals, all of which were supposed to help youngsters grow into strong, beautiful, intelligent and superb adults. I also very clearly remember the hype of Ovaltine. It was then very much in vogue for all of these underwriters to offer free or inexpensive premiums aimed at their young and generally very impressionable listeners. Some of these premiums were cardboard or plastic toys, packaged with the product, but others required a mailed in request accompanied by a box top or a coupon from the back of the package and a few coins. The premiums were usually related in some way to the story line of the program, like a "magic decoder" or a "secret signet ring". Often the hero or heroine of the program repeatedly made use of such an item to solve a mystery or to perform some other intrepid act. Sometimes possession of the decoder was almost a necessity in order to completely follow the plot.

The characters in these audio stories were my best friends—perhaps even my only friends other than books—and I felt that I desperately needed to have one of everything that was offered. For the child of a family that came from a country where breakfast cereals were virtually unknown this was a difficult quest. I was finally able to convince my mother that cereal was a very healthful thing to eat, and she bought it for me, as long as it was one that could be eaten right from the box, without the need for preparation. However, she and my father never veered away from their daily continental breakfast—a hard roll or two slices of bread with butter and sometimes honey or jam. My father also ate, every morning of his life, a soft boiled egg, served in an egg cup and almost ritualistically consumed, using a small silver spoon to carefully tap a circle of dents around the shell and lifting off the resultant cap, then alternately spooning the sticky yolk and translucent white into his mouth.

Occasionally my mother also ate a soft-boiled egg in exactly the same manner and would offer one to me; but I had never relished soft-boiled eggs, and I still don't. With the arrival of cold cereals I was completely absolved from joining in the egg ceremony, which, like most ritually repetitive actions, I had grown to abhor.

The radio programs began at four or four-thirty in the afternoon and continued for two hours, each episode being fifteen minutes or half an hour in length, minus the commercials. This was the high point of my day, and I anticipated each story as if I myself were about to make a once in a lifetime journey.

Usually I was alone and able to enjoy my programs undisturbed, but occasionally my father would come home early, before the radio adventures were over. This happened most frequently when Alex had an errand to do and he would first drop my father off at home.

My father's invariable priority was to hear the six o'clock newscast. If he arrived in the apartment at any time between six and half past he would immediately stride over to the radio and unceremoniously twist the dial to change the station to KFRC, the station that broadcast the news.

"News," was all he would say, never inquiring about the status of my program nor offering an apology for terminating it. I used to keep my fingers crossed that my father would not come home from work early, and I can still hear his dreaded proclamation, which always came out sounding like "Noose".

In retrospect, I am quite sure that my father did not intend to be rude nor did he have any inkling of the effect his actions had on me. He was so wrapped up in his interest in the news that nothing else mattered to him—most definitely not the undoubtedly lightweight and certainly unimportant interests of a mere child. He had no idea that the characters in those radio serials were my closest friends and my reality, nor how much they meant to me.

Although she herself had no listening preferences at that hour of the day and was not particularly interested in the news, my mother was genuinely annoyed by my devotion to the radio. She invariably found me intently fixed on it when she came home from her work and unwilling to answer her queries about school or anything else. She often ridiculed the stories as well as me for being so unswervingly dedicated to them. As long as her tirades did not prevent me from listening to the programs, they went in one ear and out of the other one. I found them annoying but there was nothing I could do to bring them to a halt short of turning off the radio. That was something I would never do unless forced to do so.

Sometimes she tried a different tactic. She would begin by telling me that I listen to the radio far too much. Then she would add, "You have it on so much that the tubes are going to burn out, like a light bulb. What are you going to do then, when the tubes burn out?"

This had never entered my ten-year-old mind. It became a terrifying prospect once I had been alerted to it. "I guess we'll have to get new tubes then," I said, already afraid that I would have to miss at least a day's worth of episodes, perhaps even more, before the replacements could be obtained.

"We don't have money to buy radio tubes," my mother said then. "When the radio burns out, that's the end of it. No more Jack Armstrong. No more Captain Midnight. No more Shafter Parker."

After that I began to worry every time my father listened to the news or Alex had the radio on for hours, tuned to a baseball game while he snored loudly in his chair. As long as Alex was in our apartment I was not allowed to turn off the radio nor to change stations. I used to wonder how much it would cost to purchase another radio, and whether I could possibly save enough from my meager allowance maybe to buy one. I stopped buying candy and comic books and all the other little pleasures a pre-teener might enjoy and began to stockpile my weekly nickels and dimes. I knew that I had to try to head off that dreaded possibility of no radio at all costs.

Although I added to my nightly prayers—I still believed very strongly in prayer in those days—for God to please not let our radio tubes burn out, it was not until many years later that I fully realized why I often felt so insecure. To this day I sometimes find myself in the grip of anxiety and uncertainty in spite of the fact that financial insecurity has not been a part of my life for a very long time.

My 1958 trip to Germany confirmed that Rottenburg is a picturesque little town with cold, white winters. Even after 20 years I could still find my way around. I'm glad that I didn't allow Hitler and his followers to deprive me of eventually seeing the old home town. Besides, seeing it again provided me with a sense of closure regarding our exodus.

CHAPTER TEN

THE APPLE RITUAL

They're strange, those little things one never seems to forget. They aren't always the most pleasant of memories, nor are they really memories at all; but occasionally something sets off those wheels in the back of the mind and it all comes back almost too vividly.

My father was decidedly not the kind of man one would call "Dad" or "Pop". He was a man to be respected for his intellect and his integrity and for his ability to keep going when it was necessary to keep going. He has been gone now for over 40 years—50 years if you want to add on the ravages of Parkinson's and Alzheimer's diseases, which left him a near vegetable during his last tortured decade; but I still remember the apples.

I guess it has been over 50 years since my father sliced and parceled out his last apple, but to this day the aroma of apples or the sound of one being chewed brings back the details of this nightly liturgy that spanned two continents, three countries and the upheaval brought about by the onset of the Holocaust.

As far back as I can remember, and I can recall evenings when I was such a little girl that I was unaware of the storm brewing over the heads of our sheltered, well-to-do Jewish family in a quiet village remote from the action in early Nazi Germany, my father's last act each evening before retiring consisted of folding his newspaper, walking slowly into the kitchen—he rarely did anything hurriedly—and bringing back an apple on a small fruit plate and a small paring knife. Later on, during the early fifties in the United

States, the act was varied slightly in that the folded newspaper was replaced by a ceremonial clicking off of the television news.

The apple, usually a green one since most of the apples in Germany were various shades of green and/or yellow, was then intricately peeled, the skin coming free in a thin, meticulous, snakelike strip, all in one piece and neatly coiled on the plate. He would then slice the apple into geometrically identical wedges, which were parceled out one by one, first to my mother, then to me, and finally one to himself. After the first round was eaten, the process was repeated again until the apple was completely gone. There were always the correct number of slices so that each of us would have the same amount. It never varied. Always the first went to my mother, the next one to me, and he would consume the third slice himself.

Although he did not begin to learn English until well into his fifties, my father was a brilliant man with a great aptitude for learning, and he came to speak the language extremely well in spite of the heavy accent he never lost. During the apple scene, however, he always reverted to his native tongue and referred to the pieces of apple as "schnitzchen"—little slices. When his Parkinsonism caused his hands to shake, my mother offered to take over the chore of peeling and slicing, but he would not relinquish his task. This was his duty as man of the house, and he continued to execute it until his illness, along with the yet unidentified Alzheimer's, mandated hospitalization and eventually confinement to a nursing home.

Nothing was ever discussed about the apple ritual. It just happened as regularly as clockwork. A moody man who sometimes went days without speaking a word to my mother or to me, my father nevertheless went through with the apple ritual even during the worst of his depressions. If he was tired from the unaccustomed physical labor our exodus and immigration had pressed upon him to maintain his family, it would take place earlier in the evening, perhaps shortly after dinner. The few times when a cold or other virus had confined him to his bed, he would get up and sit on the sofa to apportion the apple slices anyway.

I suppose my father was ritualistic in other ways, although the only other thing that really sticks in my mind that way is how he would eat his daily soft boiled egg out of an egg cup every morning. I was a silent rebel as a child, and I don't recall openly hating the constant repetition, although I often wished that the procedure might occasionally at least be varied with an orange or a banana or a peach or whatever. It was only years later, long after I was married and out of my parents' house, that I realized that it bothered me to hear someone bite into an apple, that the sound of someone crunching away at this fruit sent the kind of shivers up and down my spine that are caused by the grating of a fingernail on a blackboard. It occurred to me that on occasions I have actually left a room when someone began to eat an apple, and the pervasive perfume of apple has sometimes evoked what I can only call a bittersweet sadness in me, tinged with an inexplicable streak of quiet rage.

The anger is gone now, as is the urge to leave the room or to scream or to ask for an orange instead; but the tingle in the spine and the bittersweetness are still just a snap of apple away.

CHAPTER ELEVEN

MY MOTHER NEVER TAUGHT ME SONGS

MAYBE I SHOULDN'T write a chapter about my mother, since I have already written quite a bit about her. When I go on this way it sounds as if I blame everything bad that ever happened to me on my mother and that I really hated her. Neither of these things is true. Maybe I hated her on and off for periods of time while I was a teenager, but I believe that nearly everyone has, on occasion, entertained that kind of feeling about a parent.

It took me a long time to realize that, in her own way, my mother was exactly the kind of person I usually like very much—one who marches to his or her own drummer. I don't think I fully appreciated that until some time after her death, after I had finally managed to shake off most of the guilt feelings. I don't believe that anyone is ever completely rid of all of those.

While I was growing up, one of the main currents that constantly ran through my life was that home was hardly ever a happy place. The eddies from that current have remained with me throughout the years, and no matter how hard I may try, although home now is a far different place from the home of my childhood and teen years, I cannot remain at home for several days in a row without incurring some amount of depression. In order to avoid that, I have to go out every two or three days if only to shop for groceries or to put gas into the car, go to the post office or do some other minor errand.

There are a few things about my mother that one has to know

before one can completely understand her—or me. At least this is my firm belief, and I have now had a very long time to think about it.

Our apartment in San Francisco consisted of two average sized sitting rooms, a kitchen, a bathroom, a large walk-in closet and a smaller closet across the hall from the bathroom. Each of the sitting rooms had a wall bed, like a Murphy bed, that folded up out of sight during the day. The larger one, which was in the living room, not only folded up but the wall section to which it was attached swiveled, which placed the upended bed into the walk-in closet and replaced it on the living room side with a full-length mirror. The smaller bed in the dining room fit into an alcove and had wood paneled double doors that closed to conceal it when it was not in use. The beds were bumpy, uncomfortable and squeaky and were a pain to make. If the clamps that held the mattress and bedding were not properly set before raising the bed, everything would fall into a heap and make it impossible to close the doors completely, requiring that the entire operation be started from the beginning. Yet, because the beds were in our living room and dining room, they had to be made promptly each morning.

I had the bed in the dining room and hated sleeping in the damned thing. There was no space for hanging clothes anywhere in the dining room either, so I had to share the larger closet with my mother. My father kept his clothes and we stored suitcases and other infrequently used items in the other one. The walk in closet also served as a dressing room. It was big enough to contain a dressing table with a mirror, where my mother applied her makeup. I was not allowed to enter the closet while my mother was changing clothes. My father used the bathroom for this purpose. I either had to wait for one of them to finish before I could use the space or had to undress in the hallway or living room, both of which I always felt were sorely lacking in privacy.

The apartment was an especially disagreeable place to be when someone in the family was ill and had to be in bed during the day. That meant the entire apartment was converted into a sickroom. Needless to say, if one of my parents was ill and in bed, my activities were drastically curtailed.

It was even more unpleasant to be the sick person, so I learned to deal with most health problems by ignoring them and working through them. I hardly ever missed a day of school or, later, a day of work. My mother treated minor ailments such as a cold as if having contracted them were my fault. I learned to conceal them as much as I could and never mentioned a sore throat, headache or stomach ache or any of the other symptoms that could remain hidden. Once it became obvious that I had caught a cold or the flu there was always the expected and unavoidable angry lecture from my mother.

"Another cold!" she would exclaim. "Dumb. So dumb to catch so many colds." I didn't know quite how to take this but dreaded my mother's reaction more than the actual cold itself; so I learned to go about my business in the same manner I did when I was well.

My mother loved America with a passion, but she was very outspoken regarding the things she didn't like. For instance, she hated cowboy hats. That was always a big thing with her. She refused to go to Western movies, and when she saw a man on the street wearing a cowboy hat she would get that disapproving look on her face that I sometimes thought was reserved only for my friends and for some things I did—or didn't do. It was almost a sneer, and at the least it was a look of derision. It was always accompanied by the same brief statement, in German, delivered in an absolutely hate-filled tone of voice. "Pfui! Der breite Hut!" ("The broad brimmed hat!") I don't think she ever realized how much these hats are an intrinsic part of the American culture she wanted to embrace.

I don't know why that opinionated statement always bothered me. I suppose it was because I have never been able to tolerate mindless prejudice against anything or anyone. I was not that fond of Western movies, and only as I grew older, almost into middle age, did I begin to adopt the Western mode of dress for myself. I suppose I did that in overreaction to my mother's irrational dislike, which was just so indicative of her "My mind is made up, so don't confuse me with facts" nature. On the other hand, it may be that my love of Western style and Native American artifacts and decor is a subconscious way of proclaiming that I want to be—and am—really, truly, proudly and completely an American.

Getting back to my mother—to her, blondes were always dumb. Anyone who wore glasses was naturally very intelligent, and girls or women who wore glasses could never be attractive to men. These were invariables, and she often expounded on them. Later in life she was forced to wear eyeglasses herself for reading and close work. She struggled most of the time without putting them on.

She frequently made fun of people's names or of the way those names sounded when she pronounced them. It was always fun for her (and embarrassing to me) to say a name she considered strange over and over and to mock it. She nearly always referred to individuals by describing something about them that she found particularly deficient or unpleasant. For instance, I had a friend in high school who was a very talented pianist and an honor roll student, but the characteristic that my mother noticed most about her was that she was grossly overweight. She never referred to Dora by name or by her musical proficiency. It was always, either in German or in English, "The fat one." Another friend was a brilliant student and a highly motivated member of the school debating team, but to my mother she was never "Kleo". She was "The one with the thick glasses".

Pregnant women were another favorite target. For some reason that I have never been able to fathom she found outward signs of pregnancy repugnant. I think she felt that any woman beyond the fourth month of pregnancy should remain at home and completely out of the public view. If she saw a pregnant woman she would wrinkle her nose in disgust and exclaim, always in German, "The fat belly!" I wonder what she would have to say about today's tendency for women to nurse their babies sometimes in plain view of the general public. No, I don't wonder. I know for sure that she would have some disparaging remark to make about that.

I'm fairly certain that it is a direct result of this that I have always felt uncomfortable around women who are in the latter stages of pregnancy. I've tried to change the way I feel, but so far I have been unsuccessful.

My mother attempted to convey her love for opera to me by forcing me to listen to her sing. I hated being forced to do anything and rebelled by refusing to pay attention; but evidently a little of my mother's musical nature had been born into me. I secretly tuned in the Metropolitan Opera broadcast one Saturday morning when both of my parents were out of the house. The opera was

"I Pagliacci", and I listened with an eagerness that soon turned into passion. I was hooked. Not wanting to admit it, I said nothing.

My next trip to the library took me into the music section, and I borrowed a book about opera, which I attempted to conceal. I read it only in bed at night and then hid it under the covers. I was completely transfixed.

A few days later my mother came home from work and said that she had bought two tickets for the San Carlo Opera Company's performance of "Cavalleria Rusticana" and "I Pagliacci". I assumed that she and my father were going, and I felt very much left out. I realized that it was my own fault, but it was certainly too late to do anything about it.

Then I found out that her intention was for me to be introduced to opera. "I want you to go," she said. "Maybe you learn to like opera."

I worked very hard to control my delight and to maintain an outward nonchalance while my heart danced within me with the giddy excitement of anticipation.

The performance was two weeks away, and I do not know how I got through those fourteen days. I still refused to admit my secret conversion to the world of opera fanaticism; so as much as possible I avoided talking about the opera in the meantime.

The performance itself was memorable not only as my first experience of actually attending an opera, but the tenor who sang the leading role in "Pagliacci", an aging and not very renowned mainstay of the San Carlo Opera Company by the name of Aroldo Lindi, suffered a heart attack during his rendering of "Vesti La Giubba" and died on the stage. I was young and guileless enough to be far more moved than shocked by the occurrence. This was theater to the nth degree, and it kindled in me a passion that ordinary reality later found a difficult act to follow.

When eventually I admitted that I had become an opera fan my mother's reaction was mixed. She seemed pleased at first, but then, when she realized that my love for opera had become a near obsession, she took up her usual tactic of ridiculing that which meant the most to me.

When I became an usher at the opera house and she learned that there was no pay involved, only the opportunity to attend all the performances, she told me that I was wasting my time. Perhaps

I was, but for the thirteen years that I served as an usher I was privileged to hear some of the greatest voices in the world and to be a part of an artistic realm that would definitely have remained closed to me otherwise. I have never regretted the time I invested in ushering.

Most of my small circle of friends also were opera house ushers, and I spent nearly all my free time with them. When they fell under my mother's scrutiny she found, of course, something wrong with each of them. The young men were "fairies". The older woman drank too much. The attractive young Egyptian girl was a tramp. Speaking mostly in German, which always remained easier for her than English, she warned me that I was going to become just like one of them if I persisted in spending all my time with these people.

That prediction never came true. I did learn things from my opera house usher friends that I probably should have learned much earlier from my mother—or possibly not at all. These associates were probably the second best choice for that type of education. Learning about life from them was reasonably safe, if sometimes a little disconcerting. The true bonding between or among any of the members of this group took place only between similar types, and, although I was accepted into the informal fraternity of ushers, I remained, for the most part, something of an outsider. Most of them were music students or budding musicians. I was neither. Most of them were involved in what was then called a Bohemian lifestyle. I was not. They were free spirits, and I wasn't, no matter how much I would have liked to be.

One thing I learned during that time was that love is not always an emotion shared by a man and a woman. In our group was a tall, sandy haired, soft spoken young man who paid more attention to me than did any of the boys at school. He was several years older and worked in an accounting firm during the day. Whenever we went for pizza after a performance or did anything as a group, he and I paired off. Occasionally he and I went to a movie or, more frequently, to a local record store and listened to the latest operatic recordings. Those were the days when the larger music stores had little soundproof booths where one could listen to a recording before plunking down the money for it. We did not have the funds to buy very many, but we took full advantage of the opportunity to listen.

I was still in high school, and I wanted very much to attend some dances. Several times I invited my friend, but he always had a previous arrangement. No matter how far in advance I would ask him, he was always busy that Friday evening.

There was a woman in the group by the name of Peggy Cunningham. She later became the regular timpanist in the San Francisco Symphony Orchestra, probably one of the first female percussionists in a major musical organization. Peggy, a few years older than most of us, was aware of my attempts, and one day she took me aside and told me that I was wasting my time. She pointed out to me that my friend was not interested in going to a high school dance, but that it had nothing to do with me personally. I simply did not understand what Peggy was attempting to tell me.

"I guess I'm too young for him," I said sadly. "After all, it's only a high school dance."

She laughed. "You don't know, do you?" she asked.

"Don't know what?"

Peggy and I were standing in the walkway between the grand tier and the dress circle. The opera house was still empty, although the ushers had assumed their places and were ready for the earliest patrons to arrive. Peggy pointed to the top of the Dress Circle, where my friend's usual station was at one of the end doors. He was standing just inside the door, one hand on the railing at the top of the rows of seats. There was another young man in our set, a very blond, overweight fellow who was probably even older than my friend. He was usually considered our leader, the one who made most of the decisions. The two of them were together, chatting animatedly about something. The blond man's station was in the balcony, but he often visited in the dress circle until he absolutely had to put in an appearance upstairs.

"Those two are together," Peggy explained.

Somewhere in the back of my mind was a dim recollection of something to which my mother had once alluded and then had dropped the subject. I continued to look up at the two men, totally unaware that I was staring.

"Some day you'll understand," said Peggy kindly. "I don't think I should explain it to you right now".

"You mean I can't do anything to make him like me better?" I asked.

"I don't think so," replied Peggy. "It isn't even a matter of liking".

Just then Mrs. O'Neill, the head usher, appeared and the conversation was over. So was my dream of "going with" this quiet young man who seemed so right for me.

I also learned that idols often have feet of clay. For years I had worshipped opera singers and other classical musicians and had placed them on a pedestal. While I was an usher I became privy to a few facts to which the run of the mill music lover is not exposed. At least in those days, before the advent of the "paparazzi", celebrities had a little opportunity for privacy.

There were several attractive young ushers who were opera "groupies", although the word had not yet been coined. One of them had an ongoing affair that was renewed year after year during the opera season with a very much married, well-known Italian tenor. The others managed to score with several of the opera stars. It was a rude awakening for me when I repeatedly saw these things happen. In a way this contributed to the slow but certain collapse of my dream world. I was devastated then, but now I realize that it was a good thing, since it forced me to begin to have a real life.

As much as my mother wanted me to love music, she derided rather than encouraged any attempts I made at learning an instrument. I desperately wanted to be able to make music, while I knew perfectly that I had no talent for it. I have no natural voice and lack the good coordination necessary to play piano or any other instrument very well. In junior high school I had the opportunity to learn to play the clarinet and to participate in the school's marching band. I signed up for it, happily expecting my parents to be overjoyed.

My father, who had little interest in such things, nodded his head and agreed that it was a better choice than to attempt to join the choir. My mother did not fully understand what a marching band does.

"We don't buy you a clarinet," she said when I had announced the happy news. "We have no money for that." She proceeded to go into the usual details of our financial situation and why we could not spend money wastefully.

I had already researched the issue. "You don't have to," I told her. "I can use one of the school's instruments. I can even check it out to take it home to practice."

The school's tarnished metal clarinets were not great instruments and most of them appeared to have been through the wars. I had the intention of doing so well with my lessons that eventually my parents would be proud of me and would buy me a good wooden clarinet.

My mother and father suffered through the squeaking and squawking stage as I learned to control the reed mouthpiece and began to make more acceptable sounds, but it did not take long to realize that an hour a day of group instruction and band practice would not make a musician out of me—nor would anything else. However, after a few months I asked if I might take some private lessons.

"Clarinet is not an instrument for a girl," my mother informed me.

I was not surprised at her response but was disappointed anyway. In spite of everything, I stuck with the marching band and later the school dance band for the three years I was at John Swett Junior High. I knew that my playing was not very good and would most likely not get much better, but I enjoyed my brief crack at attempting to make music anyway.

There was a wonderful trumpet player in the junior high band, a slight, very dark African American boy by the name of Ted Kelly. I envied his talent and often hung around when he and some other boys, most of them black, engaged in an informal jam session. I had never heard such music before, and it left a lasting impression on me. I tried to explain this to my mother, but the only comment she would make was, in German, "The black ones! Pfui!" She would never have admitted to an accusation, however, of being prejudiced.

Once a year the San Francisco schools held a competition for marching bands. John Swett never did well, but it was always a big event for the band members. Most of it took place downtown, close to where my mother worked. One year I asked her if she would like to attend.

"Do you play a solo?" she asked, knowing the answer as well as I did.

"It's a band concert," I replied. "There are no solos."

She reverted to German, a practice I had grown to detest. "Can you be heard over the other instruments?" she asked.

"No. I play second clarinet," I answered.

"Then why should I go? I have to go to work to earn money."

That was all there was to it. I had hoped to make her proud of me for trying to be a musician even when I had so little with which to work.

When I entered high school, I either failed the audition for the school orchestra or, always afraid of failure, was afraid to even try. I don't remember the exact details. My career as a clarinetist ended except during two months of summer school my first year as a high school student. I signed up for a summer session that allowed me to take a music appreciation course and to play in a sadly deficient but enthusiastic symphony orchestra made up mostly of youngsters who could not make the grade in a regular school orchestra. After that funds for public education became tighter and the San Francisco school system no longer provided instruments for those who did not own them. That ended my active participation in the musical world.

Nearly everything I did netted the same type of response from my mother. If it was not going to make me money or find me a good husband it was a waste of my time. When I took up photography I was told that this was not a proper occupation for a woman. My interest in animals, of course, had long been drawing taunts. At one point I was so upset by the constant mockery that I packed up my growing collection of animal books and hauled them off to sell them to one of the city's then plentiful used book stores, a snap decision that I regretted soon afterwards and do to this day.

At first she was quite proud of my writing ability, but she had no clue how to encourage me to cultivate it. Eventually she began to chide me for wasting so much time at the typewriter unless I could sell the products of my efforts. As a youngster, of course, I had no idea how one could become a professional writer. All I knew was that I had an urge to put my thoughts on paper. More often than not, what came out of my typewriter was more than mere thoughts. It was my heart and soul. I could express myself much more freely on paper than with the spoken word.

One very embarrassing incident resulted from my early

preoccupation with writing, and it is one that I probably shall never forget. During the height of World War II, in the early 1940s, I wrote a short humorous sketch of the type that would later have been a welcome addition to one of the comedy variety series that were popular on early television. It involved a meeting of the three Axis leaders—Hitler, Mussolini and Hirohito—as they were losing the war and blaming each other for the monumental defeats at the hands of the Allies. As I remember it, the short play was extremely funny and very insightful for having been written by one so young. As I usually did at first, I ran to my mother with the just completed writing and urged her to read it immediately.

"Very good," she said, practicing her heavily accented English. "You have to get it printed."

That idea appealed to me. "Where?" I asked. I had no idea what to do with it.

My mother looked thoughtful for a minute. I don't know whether she, too, had no inkling or if she really believed that her answer was fitting. In any case, one of the big differences between my mother and me was that she would always jump in, right or wrong, with some kind of answer. By contrast, I rarely spoke unless I was sure of the accuracy of my statement.

"In the newspaper," she said. "You have to take it to the Examiner and ask them to print it."

The newspaper did not seem like an appropriate showcase for my droll skit. "I don't think they put things like that in the paper," I said. "It's a play."

"So! You want to go to Hollywood? You can't go to Hollywood. If you want to be a writer you have to get it printed so people can read it or it isn't worth anything. Go and sell it to the Examiner. They print lots of things in the newspaper."

I somehow knew that the San Francisco Examiner was far from the right place for a twelve year old to go to try to sell a comic theatrical piece, but my mother had spoken. To argue with her would be futile. Maybe she really thought that the Examiner would pay me a few dollars for my work. Maybe she simply wanted me to learn that merely writing something was of little or no value. Whatever was in her mind, she insisted that I make a neat copy of my play and take it to the Examiner offices.

To give credit where credit is due, the Examiner people could have been very rude and nasty to this stupid little girl who brought in her childish masterpiece for publication in their sophisticated daily paper; but they were very kind. I was more than a little apprehensive as I walked gingerly to the information desk and explained that I had written something for the paper. The woman looked at me a little strangely, but she sent me to see someone on the second floor, pointing to the bank of elevators across from her desk. I dutifully went upstairs, talked to two different women and was ushered by the second one into a large, well lit office. The man behind the big, cluttered desk was in his shirtsleeves, his tie loosened and his sleeves rolled up.

"This young lady has written something she wants you to read," the woman said. She probably winked at the man, but I was not aware of it.

The man looked tired, but he managed a smile. He reached out for the papers in my shaking hand. He skimmed over them, then patted them down on top of the other papers on his desk.

"You have the original of this at home?" he asked.

I nodded.

"Good. I can't promise you anything, but I'd like to keep this for a while. I see you have your name and address on it. You'll hear from us."

I never did, of course, and my discomfiture over this idiotic scene continued to increase over the years. Sixty years later I still operate in dread of rejection and have a permanent tendency to equate rejection with making a fool of myself.

Somehow, after I married Don Barber in 1959 the things I did were suddenly right as far as my mother was concerned. My many photographs became beautiful, my love for animals was engaging and my friends were no longer the riffraff they had previously been. My once preposterous activities became splendid adventures, and my mother even began to show a real interest in them.

I think it all came too late. Although I visited her as often as possible and enjoyed the lunch or dinner we had together, I was never able to feel very close to my mother. As an adult, I did not confide in her no matter how much I felt that I needed to talk to someone. I do not believe that she was ever aware of our lack of intimacy. When Don and I moved to Southern California in 1975,

500 miles away from San Francisco, we communicated once or twice a month by mail or by telephone. I visited once a year and stayed for two or three days. After she had a stroke in 1977 we moved her to Southern California into a retirement home near us, in Hemet. Until nearly the very end my mother, like I myself, loved San Francisco. In fact, she was very much like that many-faceted city—beautiful but flawed.

My mother's passing was, in spite of her very long illness, a shock—and one that seemed to grow over the weeks and months after she died. It had not been unexpected. She had been losing touch slowly over the last two or three years of her life. The death certificate read "Heart failure due to respiratory failure due to profound dementia". It had come almost as a blessing, as she had never really rallied after her first massive stroke. At times she had seemed to improve, and then she would have another stroke. She must have had a dozen between 1977 and her death in 1991, each time losing another function or two. She did not want to live that way. Her beauty and her singing ability were long gone, and she was no longer able to command the admiration and flattery to which she had been accustomed since her childhood; so the fact of her death was not completely sad. My problem was one of a monumental feeling of guilt. That, too, eventually passed and with its passing I gained an understanding and even an appreciation for my mother that I had never had before.

CHAPTER TWELVE

THE BEACH

I DON'T LIKE THE beach very much. Although I often enjoy sitting in a parked car and watching the play of the ocean, I thoroughly dislike sitting or lying on the sand, baking and sweating in the hot sun. I hate getting sand in my shoes or down my brassiere or having it grit in my teeth after it has worked its way into my food. I also don't like the games people play on the beach, including beach volleyball. I don't even like watching them.

For someone who grew up in San Francisco that may be a strange attitude, because the various beaches in that area are very popular with residents and visitors of all ages. When I was in high school, which was quite a few years before the discovery that too much sun on unprotected skin may lead to cancer, "the beach" was the "in" place to go after school and on weekends and holidays. "The beach" about which high school students spoke usually did not mean the extensive ocean beach that adorns the Western periphery of San Francisco, although that is the beach about which most people are thinking when speaking of such a place in respect to the City by The Bay. The beach that was beloved by teenagers in those days was the one along the Russian River, which meanders through a resort area on the other side of the Golden Gate Bridge, north of Marin County. The Russian River is banked by several sandy beaches that were havens, on weekends and during summer vacations, for noisy, carousing groups of high school students, some of whose parents owned or rented cottages in that area, although many made their own way there, unsupervised.

While I attended George Washington High School, during the years that it would have been most important to me to be accepted, I was never invited to go to "the river" or to "the beach" with a group of my peers. Had I been asked, I probably would have gone, although even then I had no taste for sand and did not know how to swim.

I think my dislike of spending time on the beach began shortly after we had arrived in San Francisco. I must have been ten or eleven when a tenant of the apartment building where we lived, a chubby, cheerful, middle aged woman named Sally, felt sorry for the little girl who spent her summer vacation constantly alone.

Our building had a flat roof, where tenants hung their laundry out to dry and sometimes went for a breath of fresh air during the rare summer days and evenings when the heat became oppressive in that normally ocean cooled city. Air conditioning was rare in the 1940's, and in low rent parts of San Francisco it was unheard of. Sally had first met my mother and me on the roof while we were hanging up the wash. Subsequently, I encountered her quite often. I liked to go up to the roof. The view was, I later decided, almost Parisian in the manner of my beloved La Boheme. Mostly one could see other gray and dingy rooftops, but in the distance there was a green glimpse of Twin Peaks and some of San Francisco's other hills. There was also a good vista of City Hall and other government buildings and, most important to me, the stage block of the San Francisco War Memorial Opera House. I frequently took pen and paper with me to the rooftop and wrote.

One day, I think during the second summer that we lived at 820 Franklin Street, I was ensconced on the tiered ledge that went completely around the roof. I had with me my usual notebook and was scribbling away at my fantasy when Sally came through the stairwell door with a basket of laundry.

She smiled at me, then asked, "What are you doing here all by yourself?"

It was a question I did not like to answer. I pretended that I had not heard it, but I stopped writing.

Sally was not a person who was easily put off. "You should be at the beach or the park with your friends," she said cheerfully.

"My parents are working," I said finally. "I have no one to take me." I did not wish to add that I also had very few friends, a fact that greatly embarrassed me.

"Maybe your mother would let you come with me," Sally suggested. "I go to the beach almost every day."

Sally's apartment was on the second floor and ours was on the third. The building's ancient elevator, which was located almost directly across from our apartment, ran almost constantly. It stopped on the third floor quite often, followed by the metallic clatter of the telescoping wrought iron doors. However, I had learned to disregard the familiar sound unless I was expecting one of my parents to be coming home, since no one ever came to see us. Mostly the elevator passengers for the third floor came and went to and from the apartment next to ours. It was a nearly endless procession that continued almost all night long every night. The visitors were always men, and none of them ever seemed to stay there very long. I was too young to wonder very much about that. However, it was quite a surprise that evening when one of the elevator's third floor arrivals was followed by a knock on our door.

My mother seemed startled to see Sally and possibly a little suspicious, but she invited her into the apartment.

"No, thank you," the woman said. "I just came to ask if it would be okay for Lilian to come to the beach with me tomorrow."

"The beach?" my mother asked with a puzzled look on her face. "Vhy?"

"I think she must be lonely," Sally replied. "The fresh air will be good for her, and there are lots of young people there all the time for her to play with."

I was sure my mother would refuse the offer, but after some thought she agreed to let me go. I went to the beach with Sally at least once a week after that for most of the remainder of the summer.

At first I enjoyed the outings. It was something new to do, and I still liked to watch the animated games and other activities that took place on the sand. I also had a firsthand look at Alex' wife, Rita, and her antics with her hefty male companions, although I did not understand much of what was going on. Sally knew Rita quite well, since both women were "regulars" on the beach. When I told Sally that Rita's husband was a distant relative of ours and that he frequently came to dinner at our apartment she appeared to be more than a little uncomfortable. After that, whenever we arrived at the beach Sally always put down her beach blankets and paraphernalia some distance from Rita and her intimates.

The promise of young companions did not materialize either. There were always some high school aged groups playing volleyball or simply doing what they called horsing around, but that year I was several years younger than most of them. The few children of my age level that were on the beach were there with their parents; and, although she seemed to know nearly everyone, none of these were among Sally's circle of close friends and acquaintances.

Mostly I played alone in the sand, building crude castles and primitive walls, or I went wading in the surf, delighting in the way the cooling water swirled around my bare feet. I thought of the surf as a playmate indulging in a game of tag with me. I would try but could never catch it, and if I managed to grasp a piece of it in my hands it would beat a hasty retreat.

I did not own a bathing suit or shorts, so I wore my lightest weight dresses. Sally showed me how to tuck the hem of my skirt inside the elastic leg bands of my underwear to create the effect of bloomers and to keep my clothes from becoming wet.

One day Sally introduced me to a man named Jack. He was tall and spare and had thick, graying hair. His eyes, too, were gray, and he had a long, slender nose and thin lips. He wore black bathing trunks and had sparse, salt and pepper hair on his scrawny chest. My days at the beach with Sally were the first time I had ever seen bare chested men, and I think I made a study of them. I thought then that Jack was an old man, but now when I reflect on it, he was probably in his forties at the most, as were nearly all of Sally's friends.

Jack was very friendly and seemed eager to hear about my life. He asked many questions about Germany and about the circumstances of our leaving. When he was not talking with me he watched me play in the sand and wade in the water. One day he took me across the highway to Playland and bought me a ticket to ride on the merry-go-round. I had never ridden on one before, and I relished the experience.

Jack asked me if I knew how to swim. Of course I had never had the opportunity to learn. He wanted to teach me.

"I have no suit," I said.

The next time I went to the beach with Sally, Jack had brought a bathing suit for me. He said that it had belonged to his own little girl, who was now grown up. I was extremely shy about accepting it, but Jack was very persuasive in his efforts to get me to try it on. I finally agreed to do so.

There were no changing facilities at the beach, and Sally and her friends always changed clothes by having people hold up huge towels all around them as they removed their street things and put on their swim suits. It was emotionally very difficult for me to do this, but Sally kept encouraging me and assuring me that no strangers would see me and that the holders of the towels always averted their eyes.

The suit proved to be a perfect fit and everyone told me how nice I looked in it. My complexion undoubtedly turned red as a beet, and it was not from exposure to the sun. I looked down at my new swim suit to make sure that it covered me in all the necessary places and thanked Sally's friends for supplying some privacy.

Jack led me to the water and held my hand as I went in deeper than I had ever done before. When the waves were up around my knees I felt a little frightened at the sensation of being surrounded by water that seemed to be tugging at me and attempting to suck me out toward the deep swells. The wet sand under my feet felt as if it were giving way, but the vague tickling feeling was not at all unpleasant. I took a tentative step and then a second one. This one was toward drier land.

"Don't be afraid," Jack said, putting his arm around me. He guided me further into the water. The waves were receding, and we took several more steps across the shiny sand in their direction.

When the eddies came in again, Jack held me very tightly. The water splashed around my knees, then all the way to my waist. I was suddenly more aware of Jack's strong body pressed against my back and buttocks than of the water. His hands were holding me rather firmly where in a few years I would have breasts. I could feel his breath on the back of my neck. All at once the rising water was nearly forgotten, and all I could think of was that, somehow, what Jack was doing was not right. What I was doing was not right either. Was it possible that this was what my mother had meant when she had told me never to let a man touch me, that when a man touched a woman she could have a baby?

"I want to go back," I managed to say.

Jack argued with me, but I was able to work myself loose from his grasp. I ran back to where Sally was sitting on her blanket as quickly as I could go with the wet sand and swirling water grabbing at my feet.

I never went to the beach again with Sally. I knew that Jack was her good friend, and I was afraid to say anything about what he had done. Now, whenever I think about the incident, I feel that maybe she already knew. I was afraid to tell my parents about it too, and for several nights I included in my prayers a very emotional plea that I would not have a baby because of what I had done with Jack.

A few days later I finally was able to do some research at the library. I learned that it takes nine months for a woman to have a baby and that her condition often did not become visually apparent until several months after the action that caused it. The books available to me did not describe the sex act itself and how it was done, nor did they go into much detail about the results of the act and how those results manifested themselves. I could find nothing in those volumes to calm my rampant fears regarding what had occurred on the beach that day. It was not until about six months afterwards that I finally was able to stop worrying that I might be pregnant. That was many years ago, but I still don't care very much for spending time at the beach.

CHAPTER THIRTEEN

GROWING UP

There were some other things about living at 820 Franklin Street that influenced my childhood and adolescence, and there were some people who certainly did so. There were the Consiglis, for instance.

Marie Consigli was a single mother whose lined face and hard exterior were only minor indications of the effects of the difficult life of a divorced woman with children to raise during and after World War II, when government entitlements and other handouts for anyone other than a war veteran were few and far between. In any case, Marie would have been too proud to accept help from anyone other than her handful of gentleman friends who frequently came to call on her. She took the business of bringing up her two daughters very seriously and never would have applied for food stamps or any other kind of subsidy. She had no professional training and worked as a seamstress or at other semi-skilled labor and always seemed to manage to make ends meet.

The Consiglis lived on the same floor as we did, at the end of the hallway to the right of our apartment. Besides Marie there were the two daughters, Frieda and Stella. Frieda was two or three years my senior, and Stella was several years older than her sister. At the time we first moved in Frieda had just begun junior high school, which made her feel so superior to me that she nearly always made a conscious effort to completely avoid me, as if I didn't even exist. Stella was old enough to be more understanding and at least greeted me with a friendly smile on the few occasions that we met in the hallway or in the elevator.

Stella was, as I remember her, extremely beautiful, with dark, Italianate eyes and jet black hair. Frieda's coloring was lighter, and she was rather plain. Both girls were avid ice skaters, a sport that was reasonably accessible to working class children whose parents were able and willing to make the necessary financial sacrifices to provide skates, rink time and lessons. In the forties the aura of Sonja Henie's fame had made ice skating the cultural sports activity of choice among parents of middle class status or below, supplanting ballet lessons or gymnastics for their children.

Winterland, a large and popular ice arena, was within twenty or twenty-five minutes' walking distance from the apartment house on Franklin Street. It was not a place where I usually wanted to be. Only the "in" people from school hung out there even just to watch.

My mother's friendship with Marie Consigli started off quite tentatively. The Consiglis were Italian, which at first was reason for my mother to look down on them; and the fact that Marie was divorced was another blemish. I sometimes heard my mother making comments to my father about the men who called on Marie and the type of woman she must be. I did not understand most of what was being said, and my only opinion was that I did not like Frieda very much. I had no feeling one way or another about Marie and Stella. Eventually my mother and Marie became friendly, and Marie even helped my mother obtain her first real employment, at the Nancy Ann doll factory, where Marie herself had worked for many years as a seamstress.

I was probably about 14 years old when I became completely aware of how much time the two Consigli girls spent at Winterland, and one day I learned that Stella, who had been working as a secretary for several years, had been signed to a contract by the Ice Follies. It was a very exciting time for the three Consigli women, and they held an impromptu party in their apartment to celebrate the momentous occasion.

As detached as I felt from any kind of sports, I could not help but admire Stella's success and the talent and ability she must have possessed. I had never seen her skate, but in my dream world I saw her immediately as a star, like Sonja Henie, skating not only over the ice of rinks and arenas all over the world but into films and then into the hearts of thousands of adoring fans. In my mind I saw her picture, larger than life, on posters, her attractive features radiant as she figure skated in magnificent costumes, her dark hair cascading in carefully managed curls over her shoulders. For the first time that I could remember I wanted to attend a performance of the Ice Follies.

Stella's contract, of course, was for her to skate in the chorus, and she toured with the Follies in that capacity for maybe two or three years. Whenever the show came back to San Francisco Stella always spent her nights at her mother's apartment. Often she arrived in front of the house in an expensive car and was escorted upstairs on the arm of a handsome and well-dressed man. Maybe I remember her life as being more glamorous than it actually was, but she was the only star I knew personally. Even her name meant star, and I was very much impressed.

The biggest impact Stella Consigli made on me, however, came one day while the Ice Follies were on tour somewhere in Southern California. I do not remember how I first heard about it, but the surprise came suddenly and, to my knowledge, without any previous warning. Stella unexpectedly announced her decision to leave the Ice Follies and to enter a convent to become a nun.

Nearly everyone thought that there must have been a man and a devastating love affair involved, but Stella insisted that there was no such occurrence. She claimed that she had received a calling or vocation, or whatever that inner urge might be; and she could not be persuaded away from her decision. Not long after she had revealed her intentions Stella entered a Catholic convent in the Los Angeles area and became Sister Marie Gertrude.

The Consiglis had always been practicing Catholics, but they had never given the impression of having any more than an average adherence and devotion to their faith. Both Marie and Frieda seemed to be as completely incredulous as those who were outside the family. Each of them made several trips to Los Angeles and eventually returned convinced that Stella had found her true mission in life.

A few years later, shortly after I had graduated from high school and had begun working, I satisfied my own need to visit Sister Marie Gertrude and rode the Greyhound bus to Los Angeles. I did not understand such things at the time nor do I understand them completely now, but even then I had a natural curiosity about them. My conversation with the Ice Follies star who had become a nun was of necessity brief, but I felt an uncommon sense of peace as I listened to her tell me of her calling and of her new life.

In the apartment directly below us lived a quiet, middle aged, rather unattractive single woman. Miss Citron wore horn-rimmed spectacles and kept her salt and pepper hair pulled back in a tight, severe bun. My mother referred to her as "the old maid" and found it very amusing and clever to talk about her as "Miss Lemon".

I was always annoyed by my mother's callous attitude toward Miss Citron, since this was one of the very few people in my young life who seemed to take any amount of interest in me. I spent hours—happy hours—on almost a daily basis visiting Miss Citron, who asked me questions about myself, read to me and often lent me books. She was an excellent reader, and I always thought she should have been a teacher. I believe she was a bookkeeper. My mother complained about how much time I spent in the apartment below, and she sometimes made unpleasant comments about the dangers of my becoming an old maid just like "Miss Lemon" if I continued to spend so much time with her.

Miss Citron, more than anyone else, saw my loneliness and disaffection. I think she even attempted at one point to discuss my problems with my mother, only to be completely rebuffed. I shared with her my frustration at so desperately wanting a dog. She, too, was an animal lover; but she had come to grips with the limitations of living, of necessity, in a centrally located apartment. If she felt defeated or frustrated she never allowed it to penetrate her calm exterior.

I think I was about eleven when my teacher at the time felt that I was not doing as well in school as I should be. The problem was quite obvious and relatively simple to correct. She had noticed that I had become increasingly nearsighted and could not read the lessons on the blackboard. She sent a note home explaining that I should have my eyes examined and that I probably would need corrective lenses.

The news angered my mother. "I told you that you read too much," she shouted at me. "Now you have to have glasses."

I could almost read between the lines. What she did not actually express was that I was unattractive enough without them and wearing them would make me even more so.

It was a whole new world for me when I was finally able to see things clearly and distinctly. I probably had been plagued by nearsightedness most if not all of my life. It was almost like moving into another body and a different life when I was finally able to see things the way they should be seen.

The optometrist's instructions were that I should wear the spectacles all the time, but my mother adamantly insisted that wearing them would cause my eyes to grow even weaker. She said I should use the glasses only when I absolutely had to and that I should never, never wear them at a social event. For a year or two the old adage about "Boys don't make passes at girls who wear glasses" was so firmly ingrained in me that I actually tried to refrain as much as possible from putting them on. As I entered my teen years I finally started to realize that being a parent did not necessarily convey total wisdom. I began to ignore my mother's advice and put my glasses on as soon as I had closed the apartment door behind me.

CHAPTER FOURTEEN

THE DERMATOLOGISTS

I THINK MY MOTHER was far more disturbed by my adolescent acne than I ever was. She dragged me from one doctor to another, and I probably had every known treatment for the disorder plus a few experimental ones. I received ultra-violet rays and was given enough x-ray doses that it is a miracle that I did not wind up with skin cancer or leukemia. I was put on diets and not allowed to eat various delicious food items that most other people could consume without repercussions. I received vitamin therapy. There were endless medicated soaps with which to scrub my facial skin. I was given ointments of every conceivable type from clear liquids to be dabbed on with cotton swabs three times a day to a sticky salve that was to be rubbed into the skin until it disappeared. Some of these potions left me smelling like an infirmary. Others stank to high heaven of things like creosote or worse and nearly made me sick to my stomach. All of these treatments had one thing in common. None of them worked. From the time I experienced my first menstrual cycle until I was well into my mid-twenties I was cursed with horrendous rashes of pimples, blackheads, oily skin and various other blemishes.

    I was told by some doctors that I was not spending enough time and effort on my personal grooming, which I did not understand at all, nor was it explained to me. I could only assume that they were telling me that I was dirty. I washed every day, so I could not understand how that could be. One doctor claimed that I must be allergic to chocolate. Another thought it to be nuts—especially walnuts. Subsequently I was deprived of the joys of both of these treats. I did not mind giving up the nuts, but to grow up without chocolate was almost more than I could bear. The sacrifice was particularly onerous when it became quite clear that it was not helping at all with my appearance.

In spite of the deprivations and the attempts to counteract the insults to my skin by extra cleanliness, the pimples still erupted. Sometimes my mother told me that it must be the obstinacy and nastiness within me finally finding a new way to come out. I think I almost began to believe her and became, if possible, even more shy and introverted, withdrawing from contact with my peers as much as I possibly could.

When one dermatologist failed to cure my acne he would recommend another, and so it went on down the line. I believe I became familiar with every medical building in San Francisco and spent a good part of my after school time riding busses and street cars to get to these abhorred places. I considered it to be a huge waste of money and, even more than that, a total waste of my time. I must have reached my late teens before I began to believe what one erudite physician had told us—that in time I would outgrow the problem.

Just when I had begun to relax because I was certain that every skin specialist in town had seen me my mother gave me yet another name and telephone number to try. This was a woman doctor who had come highly recommended by a physician who had been treating my Aunt Gretel for one of her multitude of health problems. I did not want to go to her, but my mother insisted. I dutifully, if reluctantly, phoned and made an after school appointment.

Dr. Mossheim was a squarely built woman with short, very curly gray hair and a plain but strong face. She wore no makeup and looked very severe and businesslike in her white lab coat and steel rimmed glasses. She spoke with authority and with conviction. I found her a little intimidating at first, but after half an hour or so I suddenly came to the realization that she understood me and was even anticipating some of my answers, apparently quite aware of things about me that I had not yet told her.

"How old are you?" she began.

"Seventeen."

"What year of school are you in?"

"Senior."

"How long have you had this acne condition?"

"Since I was about thirteen."

She was not even making notes. She continued to ask about my school experiences, about my grades, my friends, my plans for the future, my relationship with my parents and even about my childhood. She asked for far more information than any of the previous doctors had done. I was uncomfortable with a few of the questions and even more so, once I realized it, with the answers.

"Have you ever been to a psychologist?" she finally asked.

I shook my head.

Dr. Mossheim picked up a pad and scribbled a few lines on it. She tore off a sheet and handed it to me. "Give this to your mother," she said. "I want her to take you to see this man."

I looked at the paper she had given me. It looked like the illegible scrawl of most doctors' prescriptions, but it was a name, address and telephone number.

"Another doctor?" I asked, undoubtedly showing my displeasure.

"Psychologist."

I looked at her, expecting more. She had not physically examined me beyond a rather cursory look at my blemished face.

The serious visage creased into a vague smile. "That's all," she said. "Tell your mother to call me and I'll explain."

When I gave my mother the note and reported on my session with Dr. Mossheim, she regarded me quizzically, as if she felt I had omitted something from my narrative. "Vhat did she say about the pimples?" she asked, the increase in her accent confirming that she was not pleased.

I shook my head. "Nothing," I replied. "She said for you to call her."

"And this doctor?" She indicated the slip of paper. "Who is he?"

"He's a psychologist."

"A psycholochist! Vhy?" Her face began to portray her frequent and familiar look of disgust.

"She wants me to go to a psychologist, that's all."

I could tell from the way her mouth tightened that my mother was angry. She crumpled the note. "I call her tomorrow," she said.

I did not hear the call my mother made to Dr. Mossheim,

but she appeared to be upset again the following evening. Dr. Mossheim wanted my mother and me to come to her office together, and an appointment had been made to go there the following Saturday morning. Neither of us really wanted to spend precious weekend time that way, but my mother's obsession with my complexion was strong enough that I knew we would follow through.

The interview was brief. After a perfunctory greeting, Dr. Mossheim suggested that I wait outside.

"No," my mother said curtly. "Ve have nossing to talk." When she became angry and was forced to speak English, my mother's accent always broadened dramatically. It embarrassed me.

"I think your daughter needs to see a psychologist," Dr. Mossheim said quietly. "She has some emotional problems."

My mother's dark eyes blazed. "My daughter is not crazy," she shouted. She grabbed me by the arm and piloted me toward the door. "Sat is all."

On the way home, as we sat on the hard, uncomfortable seat of the nearly empty streetcar, I tried to explain to my mother that Dr. Mossheim had not intimated that I was insane, that there was a vast difference between a psychologist and a psychiatrist; but she would hear none of it. She was still filled with anger and continued to denounce Dr. Mossheim as well as Aunt Gretel's doctor who had recommended that we go to her, ending with the, to her, profound statement that women were not meant to be doctors. I had to bite my tongue to keep from telling her how I felt about that narrow-minded and completely asinine idea.

The one good thing that came of the meetings with Dr. Mossheim was that apparently there were no more skin specialists remaining for me to visit. In time the worst of the acne disappeared, although my skin has never been one of my better features. Undoubtedly quite a few of the moles and other spots I have now can be attributed to some of the multitude of failed attempts to cure my acne. I probably am lucky that I don't have anything much worse than bad skin, thanks to the at that time not well understood ultra-violet, x-ray and whatever other lamp treatments to which I was subjected.

CHAPTER FIFTEEN

RELIGION

I HAVE SAID VERY little about my religion other than the obvious fact that I was born to Jewish parents. For the greater part of my life I have been an agnostic. I don't feel that I know enough to be able to say definitively that there is no God. There are times when I pray, just to make sure I've covered all the bases. I genuinely admire people who have true faith and live by it; but that isn't for me.

Other factors of my Jewish background are also quite lacking. Believe it or not, I did not even know what a Klezmer band was until I was into my sixties and a friend explained it to me. I thought that I would at least have a fair exposure to the musical element of Jewish tradition. Folk songs, religious music and horas, yes. Klezmer—no.

My father, at the time of his marriage to my mother, was a practicing Orthodox Jew. He had been brought up to observe most of the laws and traditions of the faith, although some of his religious practices and beliefs had been eroded by his experiences in the German army during World War I as well as the innate difficulties of following a demanding minority denomination while involved in trying to live a mainstream lifestyle.

The Horkheimer family, on the other hand, was not at all religious. As a young girl my mother had actually attended a Catholic school, the best private educational facility that had been available nearby, which her family had considered far more important than a religious background and schooling. Although the Horkheimers did not observe the kosher laws and rarely attended synagogue, they did not eat pork or bacon. Somewhere during her adolescence or early adulthood my mother had got it into her head that ham was not quite as evil as the other two examples of pig's flesh; so it was permitted while I was growing up to eat ham—but not bacon or pork. I still think of that as rather a charming attribute of my mother's persona.

I am not certain at what point my father completely ceased to follow his Orthodox heritage. It may have been during and as a result of his experiences during the Hitler regime, but most likely it began much earlier than that. As far back as I can remember religious worship was not a cornerstone of our family life, although my parents wanted me to be educated in the Jewish faith.

From the time we settled in San Francisco until I was well into my teens I was forced to attend Sunday school at the synagogue where Alex and my family spent the High Holidays. As with most things that I was told that I *had* to do, I was not given a reason why—so I rebelled and sat through Sunday morning classes week after week without paying much attention. In those days I could daydream entire novels when I was bored with what was going on around me, an ability I sometimes wish had not faded with the years. Occasionally my Sunday school instructor gave me a note to take home to my parents about my inattention and passive hostility, but these somehow never reached their intended audience. Eventually I learned that I could spend Sunday mornings window shopping near the synagogue, going home at the time I would get there had I actually attended class. Several years later I went to the library and read myself a crash course in being Jewish—set off by a preposterous infatuation with a new cantor in town who moonlighted as an opera singer! That was an incredible phase in my life and one that I recall with a bittersweet mixture of memories.

My mother never really understood that once the money was gone everything was changed. She was a snob without anything about which to be such an elitist. She looked down on Jews from countries other than Germany and asserted emphatically that only lower types spoke Yiddish. However, in time I realized that words like "tochus" and "ferkakta" and "schlemil" sometimes found their way into her conversation. Although she considered none of my friends, male or female, ever to be good enough for me, she criticized my appearance nearly constantly along with what she perceived as my lack of mate seeking interests and my failure to go where I could meet a nice Jewish doctor or dentist or lawyer for eventual matrimony. For a short time I dated a very Jewish looking college student who was working his way through school as a Watkins distributor but had the intention to become an attorney. She really pushed me to establish a good and lasting relationship with Joel (he looked a little like Woody Allen, and I think that probably is one reason I cannot to this day abide Woody Allen or his films) because he was a "nice" Jewish boy with a proper future. Joel was a whiny voiced wimp with clammy hands that I had to keep removing from various parts of my anatomy whenever we went to a movie or anywhere else that was even partially removed from public view. His favorite pastime, since it was as far as I would go, was to park his beat up and rusty station wagon at some lovers' lane—usually Twin Peaks—and clumsily explore my entire body with his soft, damp hands. In spite of my mother's pressure—or perhaps partly because of it—I found him quite repulsive.

I never could explain to my mother that almost invariably "nice" Jewish doctors, dentists and attorneys or young boys whose ambition it was to become one of those sought Jewish girls who came from well to do families that could contribute materially to their future careers. There were exceptions, of course; but these were always girls, not necessarily Jewish, who were gorgeous and or who had "it", as the saying went in those less sophisticated years. "It" referred to a definite but undefinable sexual attractiveness and personal magnetism that I could recognize in others but certainly did not possess myself. My mother always considered it my fault that I did not meet the "right" boys. Perhaps it was. I persisted in following my own drummer in almost every way that was available to me. At any rate, her definition of the right boys did not match mine at all.

When it came to interaction with the opposite sex I definitely was a late bloomer. I did not begin really dating until I was out of high school. I did have a few Jewish boyfriends over the years, but by the time I had reached my late teens religion—neither mine nor that of my boyfriends—was definitely not a priority with me.

From the time I was a sophomore in high school I worked

evenings as an usher at the War Memorial Opera House. It was a position I prized beyond everything else in my world, as I had not only inherited my mother's familial love of classical music but had become a rabid opera fan. In order to obtain the job I had to lie, as the openings for ushers were available only to music majors. I had no talent in that direction and was not enrolled in any music courses; but I realized that this was not an occasion for truthfulness. I devoted many years to ushering and stayed on long after I had graduated from high school and had started working at a regular job in the daytime.

As an opera house usher I had unlimited access to all the magnificent music I would otherwise not have been able to afford to hear. I also was finally able to meet some kindred souls and to finally form some meaningful friendships.

One of the people I encountered while ushering was an Israeli exchange student by the name of Nahoum Boyardsky. Nahoum was one of a group of young people who were studying at the University of California at Berkeley. He and three others—two young men and a girl—quite regularly came to the opera house to usher. I was quite taken with one of the other boys, a very handsome, muscular young man with a wonderful smile and a scintillating, outgoing personality. Nahoum, on the other hand, was quiet and secretive as well as gaunt and somewhat mousy looking. The other boy, much to my dismay, was quite wrapped up with the Israeli girl, who was similarly attractive and personable. Nahoum, once introduced to me and aware of my background, attached himself to me.

For a while I found him to be interesting company, with his exciting stories of the emerging young nation in which he had grown up. I went out with him several times, always to museums or to the zoo. Admission to these was still free to the public then, and it was obvious that Nahoum had no disposable money to spend on entertainment. I paid for pizza or sandwiches on our dates, an arrangement with which Nahoum was far more comfortable than even an impoverished American college student would have been. I did not find him physically attractive, and our relationship never progressed beyond holding hands and an occasional hug or quick, dry peck on the lips. We double dated with the good looking one and the Israeli girl or with the third Israeli boy and his American girlfriend. I was very happy to be able to tell my mother that I was dating a Jewish boy, but beyond that I had little interest in anything coming of the relationship.

One evening the Israeli group appeared at the opera house without Nahoum. I learned that the police had arrested him for car theft and that he was being held in the Berkeley jail until he could be sent back to Israel. The other Israelis explained to me that Nahoum did not consider his action to be a serious crime, since he had only taken something that he truly needed.

There were a few other Jewish men and boys in my life, including my first true love, whom I lost to his mother. One of the few times my mother was totally right about one of my relationship problems involved this one. She warned me that he was a "mama's boy" and because of that would never make me happy. The other one with whom I had a close relationship was an intriguing charmer whose father was a Dutch Jew. His mother was Hawaiian. Dick was darkly handsome in a somewhat Eurasian manner, with smooth, yellowish brown skin, curly, jet black hair and minimally slanted blue eyes. He had a slim, athletic body and a fiery disposition that could quickly change from playful to perverse. Bright and funny, Dick had an excellent job and was definitely headed up the corporate ladder. I had not known him very long when I learned that he had a serious health problem, an aneurysm that occasionally blocked the blood flow to his brain. The way he explained it to me, it was a time bomb that could kill him at any time. He carried strong medication in case of an attack, a pain killer that would knock him out for several hours. If he did not take the pill immediately, he would suffer from a migraine so severe that he could fly completely off the handle and not remember a thing afterwards. He told me that he had once nearly killed his own mother during one of his attacks. The aneurysm could possibly have been corrected by surgery, but he had been advised that there was only a fifty percent chance that he would survive the operation. Besides prescribing the pain pills, Dick's doctors had warned him to avoid stress and never to overdo anything physically or emotionally. A vital, ambitious man, Dick had boundless energy and obstinately disregarded these instructions and whatever anyone else did, he attempted to do twice as long, twice as fast and several times more frequently.

My parents had mixed feelings about Dick. He was part Jewish. That was good. He was part non-Caucasian. That was not good. Eventually his restless nature erupted into rudeness while he was visiting me at home, and he was no longer in favor with my parents after that. I continued to date him until I spent a disastrous weekend with him in the mountains near Yosemite National Park.

We had been invited to visit a friend, Shirley Julian, who had married a forest ranger and lived in an isolated cabin among some of the most glorious scenery California, if not the world, has to offer. Dick was in his most charming mode when we first arrived. We went hiking, and he played his ukulele and sang Hawaiian songs to me. Then he taught me how to shoot a target pistol. Shirley and Monte found him delightful, and Shirley, an ex-workmate who had seen me through several ill-fated relationships, told me in private that I had really struck paydirt to find such a great boyfriend.

All that ended abruptly immediately after dinner. One of the down sides of Dick's drive and vigor was that he had an unbelievable appetite. He could easily consume three or four times the amount of food most men nearly twice his weight would eat. Shirley and Monte were not prepared for that. Shirley had prepared a simple but tasty meal in sufficient quantity to satisfy four normally hungry people. When we had finished eating, Dick looked squarely at her. His facial expression was one of discontent.

"Is that all?" he asked. "Is there anything else to eat?"

Shirley blushed. "Are you still hungry?" she asked rather incredulously.

"I'm starving," said Dick.

I gave him a look, hoping that he would read the message to keep quiet.

"I can get you some bread and butter and honey," said Shirley. "Or maybe a bowl of cereal."

Dick made a face. "Is there somewhere to go where we can get a steak?" he asked. "I need some real food."

Monte, who seldom said much, looked startled. "A steak!" he exclaimed. "You mean you still want a steak after eating a whole dinner?"

"That was more like an appetizer," said Dick.

I was becoming increasingly mortified. I also wondered, as I had wondered occasionally before, how much of my time I would have to spend cooking were I to marry Dick—and how much of our income would have to be spent on food that would be enough to satisfy his voracious appetite.

Monte suggested we go to a local roadhouse where they had Western music and dancing on Saturday evenings. It was obvious that the Julians not only felt badly that they had not served enough of a meal but also that they really had not planned on going out. The roadhouse was nearly an hour's drive over winding mountain roads from their cabin.

Dick offered to drive, which, like nearly everything he did, he did well, although too rapidly for that type of road. As soon as we arrived at the roadhouse he ordered a complete steak dinner and ate every bit of it while Shirley, Monte and I each had a beer and watched him somewhat incredulously.

We had not gotten very far on our way back to San Francisco the next day when Dick began to show signs of an incipient headache. When he had one of his aneurysm attacks his right eyelid would become droopy. He was driving, and I offered to take over.

"I can drive," he said gruffly.

I knew that it was senseless to argue with him when he was in this condition. I also knew that it was dangerous to allow him to continue to drive.

"Do you have your pills?" I asked.

"Yeah, but I'm not taking any," he replied. "I'm fine. I'll get us home."

I was frightened. We were still five or six hours' driving time from the Bay Area. I had never seen him in the full throes of an attack, as he had always refused to allow it. If we were together when he felt one coming on, he had always insisted on leaving immediately.

"Dick, if you have a headache you should take your pill."

"I don't need a pill. Just leave me alone." His face was frozen into a mask, and his hands gripped the steering wheel of my little Hillman Minx with white knuckled intensity.

We were passing through a small town, and I suddenly had an idea. I told him that I had to go to the bathroom.

He did not want to stop, but after a little urging he swerved into the parking lot of a coffee shop.

"As long as we're here, let's have a cup of coffee," I suggested.

We found a booth, and I made my way to the ladies' room. When I returned, I sat next to Dick instead of opposite him. He was very quiet and sat rigidly. Beads of perspiration were forming on his forehead. The eye was really drooping.

"Don't you want to take your sweater off?" I asked. "It's warm in here."

Almost to my surprise, he complied, dropping the sweater on the seat between us. I bided my time, nervously awaiting an opportunity to search his pockets. Much to my relief I found the vial of capsules without his noticing my maneuver.

"Maybe you ought to use the restroom too," I suggested. "Then we won't have to make another stop."

Luck was with me that day. Dick took my advice. As soon as I was sure that he had actually gone into the men's room, I dumped the contents of two capsules into his coffee. I knew that the dosage was two, but I did not know anything else about administering the medication. I hoped that Dick would not notice anything strange about the taste of his coffee when he came back.

My luck held. He drained the coffee and drank another half a cup before he passed out. Someone helped me to get him into the car, and I was able to drive all the way home before the effects of the drug wore off. In fact, Dick was still so groggy that he willingly followed me into the house and lay on the sofa, where he quietly slept through the night. In the morning he had no recollection of the incident nor of anything that had happened after we had left the Julians.

Years later, in 1959, when I brought my future husband home to meet my mother I thought she would certainly not find him acceptable. Arthur Donald Barber was not only an American and a Protestant, although a non-practicing one, but he was also in the Navy. My mother's upbringing had instilled in her the notion that "nice" girls do not go out with sailors. By that time, though, my mother had almost given up on my ever finding someone who would marry me. She had resigned herself to the fact that her daughter, still single at the age of 27, was going to be what was then still considered a failure in the most important aspects of life—a career woman. I am certain that she had even thought on occasion that I might have become a lesbian, since among my collection of artsy friends there were several homosexuals. She had never confronted me in an accusatory manner nor directly questioned me about being gay, but her disapproval of most of my friends was glaringly obvious. She had made it quite clear that she considered skewed sexual preferences to be contagious, and I could tell that she sometimes feared the worst about me. I had been learning the finer points of photography from and keeping company with Ruth Bernhard, a well-known photographer who specialized in still lifes and very artistic studies of the nude female body. Ruth and I had become very close friends, and I was spending much of my free time at her studio. Quite open about her lesbian lifestyle, Ruth was intellectually and artistically stimulating and a knowledgeable and entertaining companion with whom to visit art galleries and the theater and to commune with nature. She and I frequently went on photographic expeditions together. She had taken great pains to explain to me the frequent heartbreaks and many disillusionments of her way of life, lest I felt drawn to it. Although I explained this to my mother, she constantly made disparaging remarks about Ruth and never ceased to make suggestions and even issued orders that I break off my friendship with her. Of course I didn't.

My mother's immediate reaction to Don Barber was that he was an absolutely wonderful man. The fact that he had brought her a dozen roses the first time he was invited to dinner at our home had a great deal to do with that; but mainly, I believe, she welcomed him with open arms because there was apparently a chance that he was going to be my husband.

Don and I were married in July of 1959, with Ruth Bernhard serving as my matron of honor. Most of my friends gave our union less than six months, but our marriage has, to this point, lasted over 45 years. Religion, or lack of it, has never gotten in the way.

CHAPTER SIXTEEN

FIRST JOB

Throughout most of my high school years I was very reluctant to face the fact that there would probably be no money for me to go to college. The thousands of scholarships now available for a multitude of different groups were not available then, and the entire concept of low interest college loans was still many years in the future as well. Not that my parents would ever have approved of my obtaining a loan for any reason whatsoever. They were very much old school in many ways, and one of them was that one never borrowed money unless it was a matter of life and death. My teachers and counselors kept telling me to stay with college preparatory courses in spite of my argument that I would most likely not be able to go. My mother kept preaching about learning to type and signing up for business classes. This was about the time the term "nice office" first appeared in my life, and I soon grew weary of hearing it. I did not wish to work in an office, nice or otherwise. I wanted to run a zoo or to do some other work with animals. Later, as I became a little more realistic in my expectations, I thought about becoming a pharmacist. At least it was a respected profession that was beginning to be open to women, and it had something to do with science rather than with a typewriter or a filing cabinet and working in a "nice office".

I did take two years of typing and, thanks to my poor coordination, did not do very well with it. Much later I realized that my problem could be overcome by lack of pressure and have become, over time, quite a proficient touch typist. Like most other things in my life during high school, typing was a painful experience in those days.

My parents—mainly my mother—constantly reminded me that my father was getting older and would not be able to do the manual labor he was required to perform at Bauer Cooperage for many more years. I would be expected to help out financially. If I insisted on going to college I would still have to earn enough money to help with the rent and groceries as well as to pay my tuition and other expenses. I could not envision any job I might be qualified to do that would give me that much remuneration during my college years and still would allow time for classes and study. Even if I could get one of the rare scholarships that might be available to me it would be for tuition only and I would still have to find some way to earn money. Most of the girls I knew who were working their way through college did so by waiting tables half the night, and they were barely making ends meet. Waitressing was not something I could see myself doing. Even the thought of it brought on visions of spilled food and crashing dishes, not to mention what my mother had drilled into me for so many years—that being a waitress was not one of the things "nice" girls did. Not that I agreed with that little bit of Jewish princess philosophy, but one can't listen to the same note over and over for so long without having at least some of it stick in one's craw. Being a waitress simply did not appear to be an option.

Of course there was no encouragement from my mother regarding further education after high school. She continued to tell me that I was smart enough already and did not need college. She was certain that I would soon marry and have children anyway; so time and money spent on more schooling would be a waste. I didn't agree with her, and we argued frequently and often loudly. My father, in typical old world fashion, stayed out of the fray. Traditionally this was a question for mother and daughter to decide. Behind his silent façade, however, I feel quite certain that he was hoping I would find a way.

My teachers and my counselor continued to refuse to accept that I was not university bound. With my nearly straight A record in academic subjects throughout high school, not planning on going on to higher education was beyond their belief. I told them that my family could not afford it, and they suggested some possible scholarships for which I might apply. All of them offered meager assistance.

When I brought that information to my mother, she responded almost angrily with, "Daddy won't be able to work much longer. You will have to get a job. You don't need to go to college to work in a nice office. You can be a secretary like other girls."

To my mother, the word secretary meant someone who sits at a typewriter all day and types. She did not understand the need for shorthand or other office skills, none of which I had or even wanted. She equated offices with typing, and I had taken typing classes in school; so naturally I would be able to work in an office. She had always felt the need to admonish me for my failure to get A's in typing, since it was such an important course. She could not understand why that was unattainable for me when I managed to get A's in everything else—except physical education, of course. I could not explain to her that the same lack of coordination that kept me from excelling at sports was plaguing me again, and the more pressure there was put on me, the worse my coordination became.

I sometimes thought if I heard that term "nice office" one more time I would explode. It was right up there with meeting a "nice Jewish doctor or lawyer". Maybe it was even ahead of that, since the threat of it was much more imminent.

Throughout my senior year I kept trying to come up with some kind of scheme that would make it possible for me to continue my education after high school. My first choice would have been to attend the University of California in Berkeley, but the cost in both time and money of the commute between San Francisco and the East Bay seemed staggering. Adding up the time for classes, time for taking the bus and the train to Berkeley, necessary study and research time and at least six hours a day for working at a job, not to mention getting to and from it, there was no time remaining for such things as sleeping and eating, not to mention my beloved opera house and any kind of social life. I lowered my expectations a little and looked into San Francisco State College. I checked out their pre-pharmacy program and learned that with all the required courses I would have to take there I could look at a full schedule of classes for at least six years. Four would have been difficult enough to face, but six years of full time school plus a nearly full time work schedule seemed completely impossible. I would certainly have had to give up my opera house ushering job, and that, to me, was unacceptable. It was my only recreation and my only contact with the people I considered to be my friends.

Only a few months before commencement I finally came up with a plan I considered to be workable. I would get a job and put as much as possible of my salary away, and maybe in two or three years I could finally go to college without having to work too many hours to pay my way and to fulfill my obligation at home. I asked the school's job counselor to help me find something.

Some of the local businesses had put in requests for trainees, and I was sent to apply for several of these positions. The interviews were always difficult for me, as I was still extremely shy with strangers—and more so when I knew so much depended on how I responded to their inquiries. If the application was a written one I managed very well. Those that required sitting in front of someone's desk and replying orally to dozens of questions left me a bundle of raw nerves.

I was not hired for any of the jobs for which I applied. I heard nothing from most of the prospective employers, but two or three were nice enough to call me to ask me to come in for a talk. The answer was always the same. They had seen my scholastic records and were quite certain that someone with my excellent marks would only be working temporarily before heading off to college; and they did not wish to invest months of training time only to have me leave for greener fields. They also felt that I would be bored with the type of job they were offering. It was quite confusing to me as well as discouraging that my good report cards were what was keeping me from obtaining much needed employment.

I don't remember exactly where I heard about Carter's Photo Supply and the fact that they had an opening for someone to help out in the camera shop part of the business and in their passport photo department. It may have been the teacher who headed the camera club, of which I was a member; or it might have been the work guidance counselor. In any case, Carter's was a small store at the foot of Market Street, near the picturesque building with the clock tower that was then known as the Ferry Building and is now the World Trade Center. The area was considered part of the financial district and consisted of many large buildings that housed the San Francisco branches of a number of major businesses, several important banks and the consulates of various countries. Across the street were the huge Southern Pacific building, which belonged to one of the largest railroad companies in the United States, and the Pacific Gas & Electric building, the forerunner to today's Edison Company. A few scattered stores, coffee shops and bars peppered the ground floors of many of the buildings. Carter's was one of them and did a brisk trade in cameras, film, photo processing and related products with the people who worked in the surrounding area. An arrangement with several of the consulates led to a good clientele for passport and other ID photos that were developed and printed in the then remarkable time of one hour—manually. It would be several years before the invention of the automated process that has made one-hour photo finishing so common today. The employees at Carter's were experts at developing sheet film by hand and making contact prints from the wet negatives, squeegeed and held flat under a dry sheet of glass. Carter's also had photographers that went out on assignments ranging from weddings to window displays. My photo hobby sideline stood me in good stead, and I was hired, on a trial basis, by the owner of the business, a pleasant, well spoken man in his mid to late thirties. I started work the Monday after my Friday graduation and thus began an entirely new and increasingly educational phase in my life.

Jay, the owner, was truly one of a kind. At the time I first went to work for him I had never experienced anyone quite like him and even now, more than half a century later, I still remember him as being unique. I suppose I grew to love Jay, and it was undoubtedly mutual, although the suspicions of some of the Carter's Photo employees and others who were around us a great deal were quite wrong. There was never anything sexual or even romantic between Jay and me—only friendship and a complete trust that I had never previously experienced with any other human being. That trust continued to grow, and in time I realized that it went both ways.

I had worked for Jay for several years before I learned his desperate secret. The 1950's were difficult years for someone like him, the son of a traditional, straight-laced, religious family. Shortly after college Jay had dutifully married an attractive woman from a suitable background—an upper middle class family that would be as horrified as his own were they to know of the double life Jay led.

I often stayed overtime to help Jay with some of the store's massive paperwork. When I first started working there, credit cards were yet a thing of the future. The store kept its own charge accounts, dealing with them manually with an adding machine and a typewriter. With computers still many years away, huge file cabinets held the company copies of all the transactions. We had a large number of commercial accounts—professional photographers and nearby businesses that received various trade discounts that had to be figured out and extended. Jay was at the store until 11pm or even midnight nearly every night doing this work—or so I had thought.

I worked for Carter's (the business had come with that name when Jay's parents had invested in it as a means for their older son to make a living) a total of 14 years, with a year off after the first ten years when I was married and the Navy sent us to San Diego for a year.

That's getting a little ahead of myself, though. Going back to my first years at Carter's, I remember some very difficult, frightening and even trying times for a shy, withdrawn young girl who was suddenly pushed into a nearly constant connectedness with the public. Part of my job was to wait on customers in the camera shop division of the business. I was very eager to do things properly, so I would take home cameras or other equipment nearly every night to familiarize myself with their use. I studied the manuals thoroughly and read every book on photography I could find. Oddly enough, I almost instantly became a good salesperson. When I knew what I was talking about I did so self-assuredly, and my customers listened to me. Soon I had a following—a string of people who wanted me to take care of them whenever they came into the store. For my part, I found that I could talk quite easily with people under those conditions—a relationship with others I had never been able to enjoy before. As my confidence grew, I became more outgoing and more willing and able to enter into friendships above and beyond what I was being paid to do at the store. I even dated a few customers—mostly with nearly disastrous results.

Jay soon realized my potential and assigned me to the professional customers and the commercial accounts. I was privileged to wait on and get to know several of the photographic world's most well known participants, including Ruth Bernhard and Ansel Adams. In fact, Ruth and I became close friends, and I attended several of her photography classes in exchange for my doing her bookkeeping and other detail work that she hated. I have Ruth to thank for teaching me the importance of seeing a picture instead of just "shooting" it. I also have Ruth to thank for helping to convince me that I should marry Don Barber. I had by that time become quite gun-shy about commitments, having gone through more than a few failed relationships.

Ansel Adams was a fairly good customer at Carter's, and I enjoyed waiting on him. He was always polite and businesslike, and eventually I even had the courage to ask him if he would judge one of our print competitions at the camera club to which I belonged. I was somewhere between pleasantly surprised and completely overjoyed when he accepted the invitation.

Jay was a bright, generous and affable man whose entire life had been wrapped around his efforts to survive the debilitating Type 1 diabetes with which he had been plagued nearly since birth. Insulin dependent yet unwilling to give up a lifestyle he desperately wanted to embrace, Jay frequently used extra injections to counteract the rich foods he loved and, even more, the alcoholic drinks he felt he needed in order to fit in. Consequently, everyone who worked for him for any length of time had to learn how to deal with a severe insulin reaction. It was a fact of life for Jay to go into these near comas and to have to be fed a quick-acting dose of some kind of sugar. Because of his delicate health throughout childhood Jay had been pampered and protected by his parents and had been handed things, like the camera shop, to try to make his life a little easier for him. Unfortunately for him, his younger brother was big, strong, handsome, athletic and very ambitious. Jay always tried to keep up with him but in the long run failed to do so. This fraternal one-upmanship even extended to Jay and his wife adopting a little girl when they found that they were unable to have a second child, like the brother, Kent, and his wife did.

Kent was also very good at making money—much better than Jay. He was a personable salesman and did extremely well. He lived a very pretentious lifestyle and Jay had a need to follow suit, constantly attempting to expand his business even when there was little room left for expansion. The more he tried, the more he fell into debt.

Money matters paled in comparison to Jay's personal demons. Jay had spent the first thirty years or so of his life hidden in the closet. He tried very hard to remain, on the outside, on the straight and narrow; but his homosexual side fought tooth and nail to come out. He knew that it would be suicide to admit anything to his wife or to his extremely conservative parents; so he began to lead a double life. Many nights when he told his family he had to work late at the store he went to the bars, of which San Francisco had a monumental number and variety even in the middle of the last century. One of his particular hang-ups was leather; so he frequented several of the bars where men of all ages, adorned by sometimes outrageous leather clothing and accessories, drank and played out their often sordid fantasies.

At first Jay would change clothes in the store late at night, after telling me to go home. Since he never left the store at the same time I did, I was not completely aware of what was going on. I did think some things were a little odd, but I couldn't put my finger on anything specific. I continued to work late nearly every night, partly because my own social life had come to a standstill and I had no real reason to want to go home. Jay always took me somewhere for dinner when I worked late, but because his father did the payroll for the store he could not pay me for the extra hours. His parents kept a firm grip on his store expenses.

Eventually he started to wear some of his leather apparel in the store. At first it consisted of the occasional brown or black jacket, but after a while he started to wear leather trousers, sometimes in bright colors like green or red. He always wore his signature dress shirt and bow tie. Some of the employees began to talk but most were extremely careful what was said in front of me. They knew that I was spending extra time with Jay most evenings after closing. There was, undoubtedly, some speculation about that.

One evening, as we put away the paperwork and got ready to go to dinner, Jay did not get up from his desk, which was opposite mine. He sat back in his chair and looked over at me.

"Do you ever wonder where I go after you leave?" he asked.

I had originally thought he went home, but for some time I had been thinking there must be something else to Jay's odd behavior. "You don't go home?" I asked.

"You haven't wondered about the leather clothes?"

In a way I had; but at that youthful and very innocent time in my life I had not made any connections. "I just thought you like leather," I said, not completely truthfully.

Jay smiled. He had a nice smile. "That's only part of it," he said. Then there was silence as we regarded each other. "You haven't wondered about me? I know some of the people in the store talk."

"They think I'm teacher's pet and don't let me hear what they're saying," I replied.

"Well, they're right about me," said Jay. He rolled his chair closer to mine and spoke quietly, as if he expected ears somewhere in the empty store and office to hear him. "I'm—well, I'm leading a double life. I've fought it for years and I just couldn't fight it any longer."

He went on to pour out his sad story—the painful need he had felt most of his life to accept who he was, to stop hiding behind what was supposed to look like an ideal home situation with a loving wife and children, to be with other men who had similar inclinations. He admitted to being weak as far as surrendering to his health problems and the requirements of his rigid family. He could, he spilled out, never be on his own as a gay man. If he came out his parents would disown him and stop supporting Carter's and, therefore, him. He truly loved his wife and children and did not want to lose them either, which he was quite sure would happen if they were to find out about him. Eventually it had all come to a head when a customer had seen through his charade and had invited him out for an evening on the town. He had known then that he could no longer subdue his real self on a full time basis. At first he had limited himself to an occasional evening in one of the bars, mostly nursing a drink or two and talking. One thing had led to another, and his life had become a continuous round of working, drinking, injecting himself with extra insulin and brief experiences in men's rooms or in cheap hotels. There was always the deceit, the ensuing sense of guilt and a growing need to tell someone. That time had come, and that someone was me.

Over the years that I worked at Carter's Jay and I became ever closer. I could—and did—tell him things I would not tell my mother nor, later, even my husband. He and I felt mutually comfortable with one another. He told me nearly everything about his late night activities, and I was always at the ready in the morning to force into him the candy he needed to recover from his insulin overdose.

When his eyesight started to fail from the effects of his diabetes I took over more and more of his work, such as stock ordering and the purchase of new merchandise. I would read mail to him and answer most of it, frequently even signing his name. I was very much concerned about his drive from Oakland in the mornings and even more so about his return home in the wee hours of the night. Some nights he actually slept at the store when he had partied too late and felt he could not manage his way across the bridge. I was extremely worried about him.

One day when things were fairly quiet in the store Jay asked me to go for a ride with him. He took me to a rather exclusive clothing store that had a large selection of leather jackets and coats for both men and women. He led me to the ladies' department.

"You're about the same size as my wife," he said. "I want you to try something on to see if it would fit her. It's supposed to be a big surprise." He picked out a three-quarter length very supple leather coat in bright orange. It had an astronomical price tag.

I put it on and looked in the mirror. The coat was certainly a flamboyant color. I had never seen myself in anything like that before.

"It's a perfect fit," said Jay. "You look terrific in that shade of orange, by the way."

It was an attention getting color I would never have considered for myself, but he was right on both counts.

When we got back to the store he handed me the package. "It's really for you," he said. "I want you to have something nice that you wouldn't have bought for yourself. If I had told you while we were in there and you were trying it on, you'd have argued with me and insisted on something black or brown."

He was right, of course; but I was speechless and embarrassed and told him that I couldn't possibly accept such an expensive gift.

He would hear none of it. "I can't pay you the salary you really deserve," he said. "Please, at least let me do this for you."

Jay's mother frequently interfered with things in the store. She and her husband had quite a bit of money invested in Carter's and she wanted to make sure that it was properly utilized. Although she knew little about running a business and less about dealing with employees she spent a great deal of time in the store hovering around people and complaining that they were wasting time. Most of us despised her. Because her husband handled the payroll and she kept tabs on him as well, Jay often could not give deserved raises or other financial incentives, which made it difficult to keep good personnel. He sometimes apologized for his mother's actions. Some of us used to find a handful of twenty dollar bills inside a "Have a nice trip" card on our last day of work before a vacation. Usually there also were twenties enclosed with the annual birthday card from Jay.

When Don was transferred to San Diego and we moved there, Jay came to visit us one weekend. He could speak of little other than how much he missed me and hoped we would be coming back to the Bay Area soon. His health was failing and it had become increasingly difficult for him to run the store, especially since he had continued to try to expand his business in an attempt to pull himself out of his deepening personal debt. He had hired a sales manager, a dynamic ex-newspaper photographer who had promised to turn Carter's around by bringing in many new accounts, a promise that evidently had not come true. Jay desperately wanted me back.

My first job forced me to interact with people, and I learned, much to my surprise, that I could be quite good at it.

CHAPTER SEVENTEEN

FRIENDS IN LOW PLACES

Shortly after we had got ourselves settled, if one can call it that, in England my parents began writing a seemingly endless number of letters to Germany. How many of them ever reached their intended destination no one will ever know, but some contact must have been made. I was never directly informed of this correspondence, but I managed to piece together a certain amount of information from what I overheard either accidentally or, more often, from a concentrated effort to try to learn what was happening to my now scattered family.

My eight year old psyche, honed to an early maturity by the conditions of my current existence, resented being shut out by my parents. Part of me, I suppose, knew that they thought it was better for me not to know what was going on; but most of me felt that I really needed to know.

The first batches of letters were written directly to my grandparents, and at the beginning there were sporadic replies. The mail in both directions had been censored, but at least there was some indication that things in Rottenburg were pretty much as they had been at the time of our departure.

My grandparents evidently were in the process of packing up some of our belongings—only clothes and other personal items were to be permitted to be shipped out of Germany. Valuables, such as jewelry and antiques—my father had a rather extensive collection of Oriental artifacts—had to be turned over to the German officials, which would be the last their owners would ever see of them. In our case, two very large steamer trunks were involved, and the government red tape for getting permission to ship these to England appeared to be endless.

Since we had been allowed to bring out of the country only as much as we could carry, all three of us were badly in need of clothing. Our financial position was precarious, especially since we did not know how long we would have to remain in England. Before entering World War II England had evidently experienced rampant unemployment. As long as we were aliens in transit my parents were not allowed to work even if they had been able to find employment with their limited command of the language; so we were unable to purchase complete new wardrobes. Toni, our well-to-do distant relative—I am not certain of the actual relationship—helped us out with a few cast-off items, a charity situation that did little for my father's state of mind. Since his return from Dachau he had been growing progressively more melancholy and less communicative. My mother cried easily and often. I felt left out and uncomfortable.

Not too many weeks had passed when the letters from the Horkheimers stopped. Several attempted telephone calls were aborted. My parents then wrote to my great aunt and uncle and to an attorney in Rottenburg, Willi Kaeser, whose services they had retained on a number of occasions, until it became obvious that he had become a supporter of the Nazi party. My mother also wrote to the neighbor who had helped when my father had been taken away. Mostly, the letters were inquiries about my grandparents and great aunt and uncle.

The first meaningful reply came from Herr Kaeser. It was in the form of a polite notification that he could not help us. He had taken a commission in the German army and was in his office only temporarily to wrap up his affairs before taking his part in the war. He did say that our family was still in Rottenburg, but beyond that he divulged nothing. It was, at least, a tiny speck of good news.

My father sent several telegrams to people he had known through his business, and there was every indication that these were delivered. There were, however, no replies. At the time we had left Germany my father's brother, Berthold, and his wife, Gretel, were living in Nuremberg, a larger town than Rottenburg and, therefore, far more dangerous for any remaining Jews. They were also in the throes of attempting to emigrate to the United States. Their two daughters, Lotte and Marianne, had made an early exodus to England. Both were in their teens—Lotte a few years older than her sister—and had found living quarters with families in exchange for serving as nannies. The telegrams also inquired about Berthold and Gretel.

Contact was eventually made with either Lotte or Marianne—I am not certain which one—and we learned that Berthold and Gretel Bauer had been able to leave Nuremberg and were on their way, by train and sea, to America. They, like ourselves, were to settle in San Francisco and their two daughters would join them as soon as possible.

Several months later a letter arrived from Maria Eichberger, the daughter of the elderly neighbor to whom my mother had written. Maria was about the same age as my mother, and, in more normal times, the two women had been casual friends. With a fence in common at one side of the Horkheimer property, they had often talked. Like her widowed mother, Maria did not subscribe to the violent anti-Jewish sentiment of the Nazis. However, her husband had been a fervent follower of Hitler and was by then undoubtedly an active member of the party.

Maria's letter was short and matter-of-fact. It began by explaining that her mother had been quite ill and unable to write. Maria went on to say, regretfully, that the Horkheimers—my grandparents and my great aunt and uncle who owned the house at the other end of the property—had been taken away by the police chief and several SS men a few days earlier. It was quite obvious that she was afraid to say more.

Tearfully and in near hysterics my mother wrote to Maria with a torrent of questions. My father said that, even if the letter were to be delivered, Maria would not be able to answer it.

Some additional telegrams were sent to Germany. One even went to the Chief of Police in Rottenburg, a man who had shown himself to be as two-faced as he could safely be. As the Nazi juggernaut had begun its roll, he had professed to be our good friend. He had been the indicator that money could buy the freedom of a Dachau inmate, even a Jew; and he had been instrumental in my father's eventual release from the concentration camp. However, even in his position he either could not or would not protect our family.

There was no reply to the wire nor to the letter to Maria, but eventually we received notification that there were two trunks in British customs that had been shipped to us by Frau Maria Eichberger.

No amount of probing either at that time or later, after the end of the war, ever completely revealed details of the actual fate of the Horkheimers. Maria Eichberger and her mother had followed them and the SS men as far as the railroad station, where they had been placed aboard a train. Maria had tried, to no avail, to learn the destination. Her educated guess, and mine as well, was that it was either Dachau or Auschwitz. We later learned that it had been Theresienstadt, the so-called "safe" camp for transported Jews. It was actually just another extermination camp. We could only guess what had happened to them there.

In 1958 I made a trip to Germany. Neither my mother nor many others could understand why I would want to go there. Most Jewish refugees from the Holocaust never wanted to set foot there again. I had several reasons for wanting to go. Mainly, I wanted to see Germany. I was not going to let the damned Nazis cheat me out of seeing the country where I was born and where, were it not for circumstances, I would have lived my life. I also wanted to try to find out what had happened to the rest of my family; and I wanted to see if there was any part of the Horkheimer or Bauer resources that could be returned to us.

The German government had made a settlement. My parents were to receive a monthly restitution payment or Wiedergutmachung (Making it good again!), for the rest of their lives. I received a one-time payment of about a thousand dollars to cover "interruption of education". However, just in Rottenburg there were two houses, a large chunk of land and a profitable factory that had once belonged to my family. As far as I was concerned, they still did.

I found the postwar Germans to be polite—almost cordial. The simple folk of Rottenburg, once they learned the identity of the stranger in what they easily recognized as American clothes, were definitely curious. Many of them spoke to me as I walked around town. I felt oddly at home in Rottenburg and yet at the same time strangely out of place.

Twenty years, two countries and a war later I could still find my way around Rottenburg. From the train depot I was able to walk to the house where I had lived as a child. It still looked much the same as I remembered it. I found my old school that I had loved so much before it had divorced itself from me. I wandered along the Neckar, the river that ran through town and, along with the ancient German country buildings, gave Rottenburg its picturesque character. I had already been in Stuttgart, Frankfurt and Nuremberg, where much of the devastation of bombs and mortar shells was still in evidence. Bespeaking its relative insignificance, Rottenburg am Neckar had not been touched physically by the war.

I had been invited to stay at the home of the Kaesers. My parents had been in fairly constant contact with Herr Kaeser since the end of the war. There had been some correspondence about the family property, about which, according to the attorney, Uncle Rudolf had been doing quite a bit of inquiring. A few months before I made the trip Herr Kaeser's younger brother, Ulli, had been in the United States for a visit and had stopped to call on us. Ulli was strikingly handsome in a blond, Teutonic way, and he had enough charm to light a small spark in me despite the vast differences between us. Ulli seemed delighted that I was planning a trip to Europe and made what I read as a tentative date to show me the sights.

By the time I arrived in Rottenburg, however, Ulli was off to the university many kilometers away. Much to my disappointment I did not see him at all during my stay; but Willi, our attorney, was very attentive as well as businesslike. In fact, Willi, who was married, was quite persuasive about the benefits of my remaining permanently in Germany. He explained that whoever chose to stay in Rottenburg would have a major advantage in taking over the family property and business, all of which had been willed jointly to my mother and to Rudolf. The other perk would be that he, Willi Kaeser, would take me as his mistress. He explained that in Germany it was more than acceptable for a man to have both a wife and a mistress as long as he could attend to the needs of both of them.

If it had been Ulli rather than Willi I might have taken him up on the offer. The two brothers were so different from one another that I found it difficult to believe that they had two parents in common. Willi was dark and swarthy as well as short, chubby and soft. His face was a middle aged, easily forgettable one. Ulli, more than ten years his junior, was tall, blond and athletic in build, with chiseled, symmetrical features. They differed greatly in personality as well. Willi was always serious, talking rapidly and, in the style of lawyers the world over, often in circles. Ulli had a winning smile and spoke sparingly. When he spoke it was with a refreshing openness.

I did give considerable thought to the possibilities offered by such a move. In 1958 my career in the United States was virtually nonexistent. Handicapped by lack of a college degree, I could not seek work in any of several fields that really interested me. Immediately after graduating from high school I had taken a job in a combination camera shop and studio. I had learned the business thoroughly and, after ten years, had become the assistant manager. This was probably as far as I would be able to go, and, since it was a family owned business, it was possible that a transfer of ownership would one day mean the loss of my position. I had made an abortive attempt several years earlier to go into the wholesale end of the photo supply business, an attempt that had ended in bitter disappointment.

✧✦✧

I had been working for Carter's Photo Supply for seven or eight years when Bob Landau, the representative for one of the wholesale distributors from whom we purchased various items of photographic equipment came in one day and invited me to have lunch with him. Bob and I had always been good friends, perhaps because he knew of my background and he, also, was Jewish. It was more likely, though, that he saw in me a responsible, diligent employee. Actually, it was probably a combination of both.

Bob's company, Ponder & Best, was headquartered in Los Angeles, and they were about to open a branch in San Francisco. Max Ponder, the more active of the two partners, had asked Bob to find a manager for the new division. Bob had immediately thought of me.

I was excited at the opportunity Bob Landau presented. The new position would begin in about three months, as soon as the new building was completed. It would be a five day a week job, unlike the retail business, which often meant working on Saturday and one or two late evenings a week. The pay would be considerably more than what I was earning at Carter's, with generous vacation time and health care benefits; and, most important, it was a step inside the door toward becoming a major cog in the photo supply establishment. My opportunities at Carter's to advance were extremely limited. Bob explained the offer to me and suggested that I think it over for a few days and then call him.

I mulled over the thought of leaving Carter's and, more importantly, Jay; but I had to think about my future, and my answer had to be an enthusiastic yes. Bob would let me know as soon as possible exactly when I was to start, so I could give Carter's ample notice. I was to go to Los Angeles for a two week training period just before the actual opening of the new office and warehouse.

An engraved invitation arrived at Carter's for a pre-grand opening of the new Ponder & Best branch, and I received my own personal invitation at home, signed by Max Ponder himself. I dressed in my best party clothes for the occasion.

The new building was large, bright and well ventilated. The offices were modern, and what was at that time the best equipment and supplies sat at the ready. Floral arrangements were everywhere. Everyone who was anyone in the camera and photography business in the San Francisco Bay Area was there. The champagne flowed freely, and there was a huge sheet cake, its icing emblazoned with "Good Luck, Ponder & Best". The crowd was large and noisy, as it always was when one supplier or another was offering free food and drinks for the retail photo establishment.

I felt a wave of happy pride welling up within me as I walked in. I would soon be a viable part of the Ponder & Best organization.

Bob Landau was pouring, and he filled a glass for me. He seemed quieter and more reserved, than was his usual manner. I thought that to be a little odd, given the festive circumstances. I accepted the drink with a big smile.

"Max wants to see you," he said. "He'll be here in a minute."

I sipped my champagne, a drink that I have never been able to handle very well.

A moment later Max Ponder burst into the room. A large, ruddy man with a round, pleasant face and receding, sandy hair,

Max exuded confidence and conviviality. He was smiling broadly. His gaze swept the milling groups. Then he saw me. He nodded, moved deftly toward one of the larger bouquets and extracted a single red rose.

"Lilian Bauer," he said, handing me the rose as he shook my hand. He had a definite German accent.

"Mr. Ponder." I had met him once or twice before, when some special new product had brought him to call on his dealers. The rose had left me sufficiently perplexed to be speechless.

Max Ponder put his arm around my shoulders and led me a few steps away. "Lilian," he began. "I have to tell you something."

Before he said any more I knew that I was not going to like whatever it was. I began to feel a little chilled, and it was definitely not the champagne.

"Lilian, I have changed my mind," he said. "This is not a job for a woman."

I felt as if I had been hit between the eyes with a baseball bat. "But, Mr. Ponder," I began.

He spoke much too soothingly. "In the warehouse you have to deal with teamsters and with truck drivers," he said. "It will take a strong man to do this."

I wanted to tell him that I could deal with anything that needed to be dealt with, but I had no chance to speak. I clutched the stem of my glass so rigidly that it was a wonder it did not shatter.

"I know you are capable," Max continued. "Bob has told me everything about you. But I must hire a man."

"But I can do it," I argued, close to tears.

He was already finished with what he had to say and had started to walk away. He smiled one more condescending smile in my general direction and said, "You don't want to lose your femininity."

Where in the hell were the anti-discrimination laws when I needed them? Women's lib and equal opportunity employment were still many years in the future. I was devastated, but all I could do in my frustration was to throw the rose at his retreating back. I wish I had thrown the glass of champagne as well.

⁂

During the three days I was in Rottenburg Willi Kaeser continued to urge me to consider staying or to go home to take care of loose ends and then come back as a permanent resident. He explained that Rudolf had been in constant contact with him and that Rudolf was almost certain to bring his family back to Germany and would then be in a position to commandeer everything. He explained that my grandparents had been forced by the Nazis to write a will leaving the entire estate to Ingrid. After his marriage to Inge, Rudolf had become a Protestant, which meant that Ingrid, although only half Aryan by birth, was not considered to be Jewish. Rudolf, Willi told me, was going to convince the new German government that the will was the true wish of my grandparents, that they had not been coerced under duress or possible torture to do it this way.

"But how can he do that?" I asked.

"Fairly easily. He will tell them that he was always the favorite. He is the son, after all, and your mother is only a daughter," replied Willi. "Who will be here to contest it?"

I thought about the ramifications of living in Germany—even post-war Germany. Rottenburg was a quiet, quaint little town that seemed to belong in the first quarter of the century rather than the second half. I could have a fine, large house that could be modernized and brought up to date. I would, without having to work for it, have more money than I could ever hope to earn in the United States. I could travel. I could study and get a university degree. I could do many of the things that had been until then out of the question. There was only one major problem. I could not face the thought of living in Germany.

After I had seen as much of Rottenburg as I felt I needed to see and having concluded as much of my business as possible with Willi Kaeser, I went on to the Black Forest to visit Maria Eichberger. After the war Maria had moved to a resort area in the beautiful region of Germany known as the "Schwartzwald" (Black Forest), where she operated a pension, the European equivalent of a bed and breakfast. I had promised my mother that I would see Maria and try to get any additional information she might have about the last days of my grandparents and what had befallen them.

I did not remember Maria at all from the time that we had been neighbors in Rottenburg and would not have recognized her had I run into her on the street. She had not had an easy time of it during and after the war, and I learned that her situation had not improved.

Her husband had been badly wounded toward the end of the war, injuries from which he never completely recovered. After coming home a semi-invalid, he had passed away a few years later. The Eichbergers had a daughter, Margot, who was several years older than I. Margot had been away at school the last year or so that we had lived in Rottenburg. During the war she had worked in a factory in Stuttgart. She had been engaged to a soldier who later was killed in the war. After that she had taken up with several other military men—at first German and, during the Allied occupation, British and American. She had borne the bastard son of an American GI, who had returned to the United States never to be heard from again. At the time of my visit to the Black Forest Maria had been left with the two year old while Margot was back in the city attempting to pick up the loose ends of her life.

The little boy was a charmer, and for some reason I was quite taken with him. A quiet and well-behaved child, he seemed to immediately gravitate toward me. Not usually overly fond of small children, I found this one to be an exception, and I spent considerable time with him. The day I was to leave the Black Forest area Maria hit me with the rather incredible request that I should take him back to the United States with me. She had decided that she wanted me to adopt him.

That was the closest I ever came to having a child. I was quite tempted to grant Maria her wish, finding myself with maternal instincts I had never previously acknowledged having. I spent the three hours before my train was scheduled to depart walking through the woods with the boy. Then I took him shopping and bought him a new pair of pants, a jacket and a stuffed toy. All the while my mind was racing through the ramifications of coming home with a child. I eventually came to my senses and bade him and Maria a tearful good-bye. I still wonder occasionally how my life would have been changed, not to mention the boy's, had I succumbed to those unfamiliar emotions.

Willi Kaeser was right. Shortly after I returned to the United States Rudolf, Inge and Ingrid moved back to Germany from Bolivia and assumed ownership of the two houses, the land and the factory. I have never regretted my decision to remain in America. It may have bothered my mother a little that Rudolf and his family took over all of the property, but I don't believe it made that much difference to her either. Like myself, she would never have dreamed of going back to Germany to live.

CHAPTER EIGHTEEN

MADO

An article that appeared in a 1989 issue of Opera News sparked a poignant recollection of a brief but incisive friendship that probably impacted my life in a way greater than any other has ever done. The article, by Morris Springer, was entitled "A Flight of Nightingales".

What first attracted my attention at a time when I was quite preoccupied with other things and had a tendency to skim over most reading matter was a photograph that depicted a familiar and beloved face—one I had not seen in many years. The picture was of the French coloratura, Mado Robin. Of course I immediately devoured the article, following which I was compelled to set on paper a story that I had been intending for many years to write.

I first met Mado Robin in 1954, backstage at the San Francisco War Memorial Opera House, immediately after her somewhat disastrous debut with the San Francisco Opera. The occasion had been calamitous because of her ill-advised insertion of the famous extracurricular super high note at the end of "Caro Nome" in spite of conductor Fausto Cleva's stern admonition to eliminate it. It was one of those damned if she did and damned if she didn't circumstances.

Before the start of the opera season, the media had made much of Mme. Robin's ability to produce the stratospheric tone and several members of the press came close to literally daring her to interject it. Undoubtedly the audience had expected the feat and many listeners had delighted in it. The ensuing fracas that involved Mme. Robin and Maestro Cleva has become one of the San Francisco Opera Company's less glorious moments in musical history.

At that time I was a stringer for Opera and Concert Magazine and had a backstage pass so that I could get a photo and possibly an interview with Mme. Robin on the occasion of her American debut. I arrived at the door to her dressing room at one of the most inopportune moments possible—just as Maestro Cleva was leaving, having vociferously reproached the coloratura for her transgression. From outside the dressing room I could hear him shouting, alternately in English and in Italian as well as in a rather colorful combination of both. It took little imagination for an opera devotee to realize what was going on, and I felt the pain of empathy at what I overheard.

My own feeling toward the matter was ambivalent. I could see both sides to the dispute; but having been a lifelong (not so long at that time—I was in my early twenties) worshipper at the shrine of any and all opera singers, I emotionally sided with the soprano while artistically agreeing with the conductor.

A few autograph seekers and opera "groupies" were accumulating in the corridor when a tall, well dressed woman appeared at the dressing room door. She looked at us somewhat disdainfully and said, in a heavy French accent, "Miss Robin will see no one."

Most of the people dispersed. There were not too many. Not having sung in the United States before, Mado Robin had not acquired a following among the hard core fans who managed to court their gods and goddesses from season to season, often invading the awesome sanctity of "backstage" in their endless pursuit of autographs, pictures, a personal word or two or just a private glimpse.

In those days I used to be painfully shy and, had I not been there in what I considered to be an official capacity, I would not have ventured to protest. Fortunately I was on assignment. However, it was still difficult for me to stand my ground. The woman seemed intimidating, but I nevertheless managed to tell her that I was from Opera and Concert Magazine and in hope of obtaining an interview.

The woman frowned at me but then disappeared momentarily into the dressing room. When she returned, her expression had not changed, but she said, "Miss Robin will see you in a few minutes."

I had no idea who the woman was. She was not one of the regular "insiders"—mostly wealthy patrons who were in the enviable position of being able to attach themselves to visiting opera stars, often supplying their transportation, sightseeing and sometimes lodging, if not a few other things.

She went back into the dressing room, and I waited, not without some trepidation.

A few minutes later the door opened and the woman beckoned me to enter. "Miss Robin doesn't speak English," she said. "I am her interpreter. I am Mrs. Paul Verdier."

Nervously clutching my camera, I looked into the room directly at Mado Robin. She was seated at her dressing table, still in costume. She had obviously been crying. However, in true show must go on tradition she smiled at me with one of the most ingratiating smiles I had ever seen.

She was a striking woman—not beautiful in the classic sense but singularly handsome, with sleek, dark hair and stunningly expressive eyes. She was rather short in stature but squarely put together like the eternal image of the old style prima donna. Above all, there was a gentility about her appearance that would not be denied. Our eyes met briefly, then she said something to Mrs. Verdier in French.

"She says you should not be shy or afraid," Mrs. Verdier translated. "She will give you an interview but not now. Can you come tomorrow morning? She is staying at my home."

At that point my heart was pounding. In spite of my love of opera and my good fortune to work for the magazine even on a part time basis I was not cut out to be a reporter. My introverted nature suited me much better for my regular job, which consisted mainly of darkroom drudgery for a photo studio and explaining the operation of camera equipment.

I managed to stammer that I could definitely meet Mme. Robin the following day for an interview. My daytime employer was quite accustomed to my sudden one day illnesses during opera season. After writing down the address I turned to Mado and thanked her. She shook my hand with a firm and meaningful grip. I mumbled something undoubtedly stupid, which Mrs. Verdier, I suppose, translated. In any case, she said something to Mado in French and the singer smiled sweetly again and patted my shoulder as I took my leave.

The meeting in Mrs. Verdier's flat lasted much longer than I had anticipated, and it included lunch, which was served somewhat grudgingly by Mrs.Verdier at Mado's request. During our four hour talk I learned a great deal about Mado Robin and nearly as much about myself. For one thing, although she spoke no English at all she spoke some German and a little Italian. I am fairly fluent in the former and, although less than conversant in the latter, my involvement with opera had enabled me to understand a fair amount. The principal means we had of communicating was a combination of what we knew of those tongues and of sign language—and, most likely, of body language. We simply discovered that we could understand one another very well. Mrs. Verdier seemed not to be very happy about our lack of need for her interpretative services.

Mado was completely devastated by the cruelty of the San Francisco critics. Much of what they wrote about her was totally unjustified, but Maestro Cleva was firmly entrenched in that city's operatic tradition, and he had made his own statements to the press both before and after that fateful opening night "Rigoletto". For the most part, the critics pitted Mado against Cleva and unequivocally took the Maestro's side. Hurt and unhappy, she was anxious for the opera season to be over so that she could return to her home in France and to the comfort of her considerable reputation in that country. She was too much of a gentlewoman to battle for her cause or to walk out on the remainder of her contract, but for the most part she stayed away from the public eye during her five weeks in San Francisco except for a few affairs staged in her honor by the French community, led by Mrs. Verdier. On several occasions I spent a few hours with her, always at Mrs. Verdier's home. I was still working on a feature article, but mainly Mado and I really enjoyed each other's company. The quiet communication between us was complete and truly miraculous.

I learned much about Mado's life as a highly acclaimed star in her native land and in other European countries. She told me that her aristocratic family had seen to it that, for the most part, she had led quite a sheltered life. She was in her late thirties and had never been married, having been groomed for an operatic career from childhood, with little time allowed for personal life or frivolities. She was, however, engaged to a wonderful but non-musical man and was hoping to be married in the near future. The adoration of her multitude of French fans and followers pleased her greatly, but it had in no way affected her natural humility. She had an easy grace and charm that surmounted the sadness her unfortunate opening night experience had engendered.

I drove Mado and Mrs. Verdier to the airport to see them off the day they left for Los Angeles for Mado to fulfill her commitment to the San Francisco Opera during the Southern California finale of the season. She had been trying to persuade me to come along, but I had to work. I told her that I would try to get a few days off and drive down for her last performance. I wanted to see her again and did not want to say a rushed good-bye at the airport, especially since I felt it would be the last time I would ever see her. She had told me that she had sworn that she would never come back to perform in the Unites States again.

I did drive to Los Angeles and attended the last "Lucia" as a standee. When I went backstage afterwards, Mado greeted me as if I were a long lost sister.

Mrs. Verdier was not far behind, and she seemed much less happy to see me. "Mado and I are going to a party," she said. "We don't have much time. She should be getting dressed."

She spoke to Mado in French, and Mado nodded but continued to sign autographs and to listen to the words of admiration from the now larger group of devotees. Mrs. Verdier repeatedly looked at her watch with evident annoyance. Eventually Mado spoke to her, and then Mrs. Verdier told me that Mado had suggested she go ahead to the party and that I could drive Mado there later, after she had changed.

On the way to the party I became aware that Mado looked very tired. I was not quite sure how it came about, but we wound up with just the two of us having a quiet dinner in an unpretentious little restaurant. Somehow, in spite of the language barrier, I knew that Mado had no desire to attend the party. I wondered how angry Mrs. V. would be about her not getting there, but Mado did not seem in the least concerned about it; so neither was I.

Afterwards, when we arrived at Mado's hotel, neither of us

wanted to say good-bye. I think we were actually unable to express the word in any of our fragmented languages. Instead of bidding a painful farewell at the Ambassador entrance, Mado invited me to have breakfast with her and Mrs. Verdier in the morning. Grateful not to have to say good-bye just yet, I accepted and left for my considerably less opulent quarters.

It was quite obvious that I was not the only one trying to postpone the inevitable. Mado and Mrs. Verdier were to fly back to San Francisco late the next morning and Mado was leaving for France two days later.

Over breakfast Mado made it known to me that she really would have enjoyed being able to make the trip back to San Francisco by car along the coast so that she could see something of California besides the two cities in which she had sung. I said that she was welcome to ride back with me, that we could arrive in the Bay Area in plenty of time for her to catch her plane back to Paris. Mrs. Verdier looked glum while Mado and I laughed excitedly. In the end Mrs. Verdier had to call the airline to cancel their reservations and we loaded all the luggage into the trunk of my Ford.

We headed north on El Camino Real, Mado riding in front with me and Mrs. Verdier grumbling in the back seat. Once on our way, Mado was almost childlike in her enthusiasm for the trip. The scenery was all new to her, and she spouted forth a nearly constant stream of "Tres jolie!" Showing her my part of the world was a sheer delight.

It was late afternoon when we reached Paso Robles, and Mado, seeing the attractive Spanish style Paso Robles Inn, suggested we stop for the night. When I hesitated, Mado immediately perceived that the Inn was probably beyond my financial reach and insisted on paying for my room. She had already bought all of the gas as well as my lunch. She would not take no for an answer.

We occupied adjacent chaise lounges in the shade of the palm trees for a while, and I showed Mrs. Verdier how to use my camera so she could take some pictures of Mado and me together. I was happy to see how relaxed and at ease Mado was, and that was how I wanted to remember her. The past six weeks had probably been among the most difficult and stressful times of her life. It was over now, and she would be going home soon.

Among Mado's last words to me when I drove her to the San

Francisco airport on the day of her departure for France were once more that she would never sing in the United States again. She added that I was the best thing that had happened to her during her visit and presented me with a pretty green linen handkerchief. There was some special significance to it, but the explanation was lost either in the translation or in the mutual tears of good-bye.

Although we had been able to interact so well in person, the language barrier proved to be much too great for correspondence. We exchanged Christmas cards in 1954 and 1955, and Mado sent me autographed copies of two recordings she had made that were not being distributed in the United States. In 1956 she mailed me a lovely postcard from Monaco, where she had been invited to sing at the wedding of Prince Rainier and Princess Grace. She wrote in French, describing the fairy tale event. The card remains one of my most prized possessions.

In 1957 a long range dream began to come true for me. I had been saving as much as possible from my quite meager salary for nearly eight years in order to take a once in a lifetime trip to Europe and to visit some of the great opera houses of that continent. I requested a leave of absence for the first three months of 1958 and formulated my plans. I would start my trip in Germany and wind up in England. Paris was to be the second to the last stop on my itinerary, and as soon as I had my reservations I wrote a letter, which I had an acquaintance translate into French, to Mado. The letter was written in November of 1957. I was to be in Paris during the last week of March. I anxiously awaited a reply, but none came, nor was there a Christmas card that year. Some of my old self doubts that had been in great part dispelled through my friendship with Mado returned. Although I knew that there must be good reason for the lack of communication, I felt somehow betrayed and swore to myself that I would make no attempt to contact Mado while I was in France.

My days and weeks in Europe simply flew. I had a marvelous time during my long-awaited trip—until I arrived in Paris. Part of the problem was that I spoke no French at all, and most Parisians, even if they know some English, pretend they don't. Getting around in Gay Paree looked as if it was going to be a hassle, and I regretted that I had allotted nearly a week of precious time to that city. Matters went from bad to worse when I learned, after checking into my hotel, that there would be only one performance at the Paris Opera during my stay—Poulenc's "Dialogues of the Carmelites"; and that was completely sold out. There were, however, several performances scheduled for the Opera Comique, and two of them were "Lakme," with Mado Robin singing the lead. I soon learned that these, also, were sold out.

It was rather late in the afternoon, and I decided to wait until the next day to see what could be done about finding a source for tickets. As I had learned in previous weeks in Rome and Milan, tickets for sold out performances were usually obtainable, at a price, from local scalpers. Often the hotel concierge could help with getting them.

I spent too much money on dinner in a nearby restaurant that had a menu I could scarcely decipher and returned to my hotel in rather a sour mood.

The following morning the room clerk was considerably more polite than he had been the previous day. "Mlle. Bauer," he said with a smile, "I have a message for you from Mme. Robin of the Opera."

He did speak English after all—and rather well. More importantly, it was obvious that Mado had not ignored my letter. What really amazed me, though, was that Mado had remembered exactly when I was going to be in Paris and where I would be staying. My letter containing that information had been written a full four months earlier. I was ecstatic—and more than a little overwhelmed.

The message was for me to call Mado's fiancé at his office, since he spoke English. Of course I did so post haste, and he told me that Mado was expecting me at her flat on the Rue Ampere that afternoon at two for tea. He explained that she was very sorry she could do no more than that, but she had a performance that evening. Possibly something could be arranged for another day.

I studied my map of Paris in high spirits and found that my destination was within possibly an hour's walking distance from the hotel. I enjoy walking and seeing new places, but I am unable to recall another occasion in my life when I was quite so joyful on my feet as I was that day. Between the very thought of actually being in Paris and the anticipation of seeing Mado again I was completely intoxicated.

Mado greeted me with a wholehearted embrace. We both had tears in our eyes as we hugged one another. The old magic was still there. We may not have spoken the same language, but we still understood one another perfectly.

I am unable to recall much about Mado's apartment except that I was impressed by its simple stylishness. Mostly I remember sitting across the table from her, sipping tea and sensing the warmth of her friendship. She asked me if I had plans to attend the opera, and I told her—in German, I think—that the one Paris Opera performance that week was sold out, and that I was going to try to get a ticket for her "Lakme" later in the week.

"Une moment," she said, leaving the table briefly. When she returned, she had a card and a pen in her hand. She wrote a few lines on the card and signed it with a flourish. She said it would get me into the "Carmelites" performance that night—and it did. She also arranged for me to pick up a pass for her second performance at the Opera Comique, which was to be on the evening before I was to leave Paris. There were a few more words of apology about her horrendously busy schedule that week, but that she would see me backstage after "Lakme."

My attitude about Paris improved markedly after the visit, and I thoroughly enjoyed "Carmelites" that night as well as several days of sightseeing. The highlight of my stay in France, though, was that unforgettable "Lakme". I had owned the complete recording of that opera, with Mado singing the intricate and difficult title role, since long before I had first met her; but I had never seen an actual performance of it.

If there had ever been any doubt in my mind about the magnitude of Mado's vocal stardom it would have been completely dispelled by that magical evening at the Opera Comique. For nearly three hours I was totally transfixed. Coloratura singing is not everyone's cup of tea, but I doubt that anyone could hear Mado Robin in "Lakme" without marveling that such sounds could come from a mere human throat.

When I picked up my pass at the Comique there was another of Mado's personal cards attached to it. The cards were slightly larger than a regular business card and were imprinted with "Mado Robin De L'Opera". On this one she had written, "Leopold—Laissez monter mon amie Americaine dans ma loge. Merci. Mado."—Let my American friend enter my dressing room.

I still have the card, and for many years, whenever my self

confidence threatened to flag, I would look at it. The fact that a chronic outsider like me could actually be a friend of someone like Mado Robin began to change my entire perspective on life, therefore my life itself. I think what my friendship with this extraordinary woman taught me was that it was not necessary to live completely in another's dreams; and I began to be more of a participant, no longer always on the outside seeking to look in.

Unlike the situation in California, Mado's dressing room and the corridors all around it were literally jammed with fans, friends, autograph seekers, family and well-wishers. It was a frenetic scene, almost evocative of occurrences at rock concerts yet to come, but she, still in her magnificently colorful Indian costume, graciously made an individual moment of time for everyone. I must have stood looking on in awe for more than an hour before the crowd finally thinned out.

Eventually Mado introduced me to the tall, good looking man in a tuxedo who had also been standing back during the height of the melee. Actually, I had already guessed that this was her fiancé`. He and I talked for a few minutes while Mado changed into an evening dress. I learned that he was a dentist and that he was just a little annoyed at having to share Mado with her public—but at the same time was also relishing it. I instinctively liked him.

When Mado had finished dressing she asked, with her fiancé's help, what my plans were for the rest of the evening. I had none, of course, other than to return to my hotel, and she invited me to come with them to a post-opera party, an invitation that, for a number of reasons, I declined. For one thing, it was obviously a formal occasion and I was not dressed for it. Then there was the language problem again. Mainly, however, I was simply too timid to feel that I could cope.

Mado understood. She asked how I was planning to get back to the hotel, and I told her that I was going to walk. I found it actually easier to walk in foreign cities than to risk boarding an incorrect bus or subway train.

It was quite some distance and Mado would not hear of it, insisting instead that they would drop me off on their way to the party in her "Petit Renault." Her fiancé` protested that they were already quite late, but Mado insisted and said something to him about driving the car if he didn't want to.

That ride was quite an experience. Paris traffic is among the worst and wildest in the world, and the "Petit Renault" turned out to be just that—one of the currently in vogue tiny 4CV's that made the Volkswagen beetle look like a limousine. Mado drove it with the aplomb of a well practiced and confident maniac. Had it been anyone else driving I probably would have asked after a block or so to be let out of the car, but anything and everything Mado did was just fine with me. She told me along the way that she loved to drive, that she found it a relaxing way to unwind after a strenuous performance.

Our good-byes were said in heavy traffic, which, fortunately, made excessive sentimentality virtually impossible. I promised to come back in two years, a promise I fully intended to keep. It made saying farewell just a little bit easier.

"Au revoir till two years," was the last thing Mado said to me—partially in English.

The following morning a messenger left a small package for me at the hotel. It contained a tiny perfume bottle in an ornate silver holder that represented a cherubic angel. It could be worn as a pin. The short accompanying note said it was not a gift but something to remind me of our friendship. As if I could ever forget!

My relationship with Mado Robin may at first have been sparked by codependency, a word at that time not yet coined; but the friendship of this very warm and extraordinary woman not only surmounted this weakness in my character but accomplished more than psychotherapy could have done to help erase it.

Shortly after returning from Europe I met my future husband, and we were married in 1959. There were tremendous changes in my life, and there was no way I could keep my promise to be in Paris in 1960. I wrote to Mado to tell her of my marriage and to explain why I was unable to come as planned and felt hurt when there was no reply. Nor was there a Christmas card in 1959. It was nearly a year later that I received a note from Mado's fiance` with the crushing news that Mado had been very ill for a long time and had eventually lost her battle with leukemia. Even today I find myself fighting back the tears whenever I hear of this dreaded disease. It carries connotations of the far too early loss not only of a splendid singer but of a sublime human being.

Here I am with French opera star Mado Robin, relaxing at the Paso Robles Inn on our way back to the San Francisco area in 1954.

CHAPTER NINETEEN

ROMANCE –SORT OF

One of the last phases of development for me was the very important one of relating to and with the opposite sex. None of my experiences during childhood and adolescence had particularly prepared me for this major part of the experience of living; and I suspect that my Saturday morning of "sex education" in the slums of London, no matter how hard I had tried to push it out of my conscious mind, had contributed to my failure to connect on a romantic basis. My mother's old fashioned approach to the whole business of sex and love didn't help. Her biggest contribution to my knowledge along those lines was the repetitive and poorly explained command never to allow a man to touch me. I read quite a bit, of course, and nearly all of my knowledge concerning the interaction between men and women came from books. Some of them were romances, and what I learned from them seemed to be good; but I learned quickly that these did not play out in real life scenarios. Some were an entirely different kind of books, the kind that usually are not kept in plain view; and the information gleaned from those was ugly and intimidating.

Regardless of the level of sexual knowledge a person may have, the hormones are still there and they persist in raging. The combination of conflict engendered among those hormones, a lack of understanding and an innate fear and shyness can be devastating. Under the circumstances it was both amazing and something of a miracle that in my mid-twenties I was still a virgin.

Maybe I should explain at this point that during the innocent years of the 40's and 50's the word "dating" had an entirely different meaning from what it has now. A man and a woman going on a date during those decades and the decades prior might go to dinner and a movie, go bowling or to participate in some other sport, or they might go for a walk in the park or the zoo; or they could go to the beach. It rarely meant that such an outing would culminate in sex, especially not on a first date. Maybe after two or three dates the young couple would wind up doing some "necking", as it was called or even some heavy petting; but there was seldom complete removal of clothing or any form of intercourse. At least these things did not occur among "nice" people.

Not too long after I went to work for Carter's I found myself attracted to a young man who made nearly daily visits to the store. He was a management trainee and a "gopher" for one of the larger companies that dealt with Carter's for their photographic needs, a bright, well-spoken fellow with his eyes focused on rising through the ranks. He was clean cut and good looking, always neatly dressed and very personable. I started to rush out into the store to wait on him whenever he came in regardless of what I might have been doing at the time. I found him easy to talk with, and I began to feel that he enjoyed our conversations as well. One day he asked me if I had a boyfriend.

My interest in a fellow employee had been going absolutely nowhere. That was the one my mother had warned me was a mama's boy and I should stop pursuing a relationship with him. I told the customer—I don't even remember his name now—that I didn't.

"Would you consider going out with me?" he asked.

It was suddenly very hot in the store, and I probably turned my telltale shade of red. I managed to smile. "Yes," I said. "I'd like that."

We went to dinner a few evenings later, and we talked quite a bit about our very different lives and backgrounds. He told me of his ambition to become an executive with his company and to be very rich. He talked about his family and about his hopes for a future family of his own, and very quickly it became obvious that there would never be a place for a shy Jewish girl from Germany in his well-planned, orderly and successful life. We had finished our dessert, and as we walked out of the restaurant he put his arm around me and very obviously managed to fondle my breast.

I tried to convince myself that it was an accidental touch, but I knew that it had been deliberate.

"My car is in the company garage," he said. "There won't be anyone around at this hour to see us." He was guiding me in the direction of the large building where he worked.

"Where are we going?" I asked. I was naïve enough not to understand his meaning.

"Nowhere," he replied. "No one will see what we're doing."

His intent suddenly struck home, and my disappointment was almost like a physical blow. Even worse was the realization that I had expected much more, or at least something different, than what I was obviously receiving. I had walked into this situation without a single thought that it might occur.

To his credit, he sensed my discomfiture and stopped short. "What's the matter?" he asked. "I thought you liked me."

"I do," I managed to say. "But—." I had run out of words.

The arm that had come to rest around my waist dropped and he stopped walking, looking at me oddly.

"So, what were you expecting?" he asked.

I realized that I didn't even know the answer to that. We parted company without any further conversation, and when he came into the store a few days later I allowed someone else to take care of him. It was a long time before I accepted another invitation from a customer.

One of my happiest memories of customers at Carter's is my recollection of Eddie Broaster. Eddie was one of the most unlikely people to have any effect on my life, but I still treasure a brocaded Asian jacket Eddie brought me from Japan on one of his trips. He was a merchant seaman from Belize, a middle-aged, muscular black man with a jovial disposition and a constant twinkle in his dark brown eyes. He spoke excellent English with a fascinating, lilting accent I had never heard before, and he was completely in love with photography. He took more pictures, I think, than anyone else I had ever known.

I have no idea what attracted Eddie to me, but suddenly I realized that this man was in the store several times a day and would not let anyone but me wait on him. He would ask me to look at the pictures he had just picked up, and often I had to tell him that I had work to do and couldn't take too much time. He would then invite me to have lunch with him or to go on a coffee break so he could show me his photos. His ship made regular trips to the Orient and he would be gone for several months. Then he would be in San Francisco for two or three weeks, during which time he nearly always made a trip of several days to Belize, where he had a wife and several children. He very freely showed me pictures of his family, of whom he was very proud and obviously loved very much.

Eddie bought quite a bit of camera equipment from Carter's, always insisting that I be the one to show him how to use it. Some of the employees began to joke about me and my black boyfriend. Eddie always brought me some kind of gift when he came back from one of his trips, and there was always a package in the mail from him at Christmas. I never felt any romantic attraction to him, but I was very fond of the genial seaman. Unlike nearly everyone else I knew or had ever known, he always seemed so happy and "up"; and the feeling was quite contagious. It was impossible to be sad or angry around Eddie.

The inevitable finally occurred. Eddie came back from a longer than usual absence and invited me out to dinner after work one day. I accepted, and we had a nice meal nearby while he showed me pictures and talked about his job on the ship and what he had done and seen in Japan and other parts of the Pacific. When we had finished eating and looking at the pictures, he said that he had something else he wanted to show me and it would require walking a few blocks. I couldn't see any reason not to go.

We walked and talked and eventually arrived at a small hotel — the kind known to rent rooms by the hour. I did know that much about life, and I was more than a little taken aback. My friendship with Eddie had been going on for some time and there had never been any indication that it could go further. After all, he had a wife in Belize, and he had said that he loved her. I brought that up to him as he held the front door of the hotel open for me.

Undaunted, Eddie grinned his broad, infectious grin and said, in his musical Calypso tone, "She does not expect me to abstain when I'm not with her for so much time."

How I talked my way out of that one without incurring Eddie's anger is not quite clear in my mind, but much of it is thanks to his good and generous nature. The question of race never came up. He said that he understood my attitude regarding sex with a married man and respected it. We remained friends for years after that incident, and he always remembered me at Holiday time even after I had left Carter's and no longer saw him when he was in San Francisco.

Another situation with a merchant seaman—our location so close to the waterfront made it the first choice for merchant seamen's identification photos as well as for their photographic needs—involved a Danish sailor by the name of Steen Scheibenberg. Steen was a tall, slim young man with a serious interest in cameras and a burning desire to become an American citizen and to live in the United States. He was doing well financially sailing on Scandinavian merchant ships, but he knew he could do better as an American. Gaining permission to live in the United States and becoming a citizen is a time consuming and often daunting procedure. One of the few ways to circumvent it is for a foreigner to marry a woman with American citizenship, and Steen set about to do just that. He spoke English extremely well and had a good education. Although he was not handsome, he was clean and neat and pleasant company. He quickly learned from one of the other Carter's employees that I was single and unattached. He began to pursue me almost immediately, very openly admitting that he was interested in marriage so that he could become a citizen. He also explained that the marriage did not have to be permanent unless, of course, we both wanted it to be. His proposal, or whatever one wants to call it, was very clearly a business offer.

Steen took me to dinner several times, and we went to some movies. We walked in the park and attended a few classical concerts. He and I had much in common, and I began to think the arrangement might be a good one. The only thing that was missing was even the tiniest spark of romance.

Like Eddie, Steen would go out to sea for several months and then return to San Francisco for a week or two. I really gave some serious consideration to his offer of marriage. Also like my friendship with Eddie, my association with Steen was not something I ever disclosed to my parents. I think my father would have understood, but certainly my mother would not. One of the things I had learned the hard way over the years of childhood and adolescence was that it was much, much easier to not try to discuss anything with my mother that was outside her narrow sphere of understanding. Certainly a marriage of convenience to Steen would have been.

Eventually Steen asked me point blank if I would marry him. He said he was prepared to go and purchase a ring that very day if I said yes. He didn't try to talk me into it, but it was quite obvious that he was looking for a definite answer. When I told him that I had not reached a decision, he nodded and said, "Okay". To the best of my knowledge, he did not come into Carter's on his next trips to San Francisco. In any case, I never saw Steen Scheibenberg again.

For quite some time I found older men much more interesting and appealing than those closer to my age. This was in spite of seeing the difficulty my mother encountered as my father, who was 18 years her senior, aged rapidly while she was still a relatively young and vital woman. At a very early age I decided that I would never marry a man more than a year or two older than myself. However, the younger men I met all appeared shallow and lacking the ability to carry on meaningful conversations. The older ones were the ones that attracted me—like the Cantor I had pursued as a teenager.

There was Joe, for instance. Yes, I remember his last name but for obvious reasons I will leave it out. Joe was the manager of a company that did commercial and x-ray photography, made Xerox copies for businesses and performed a number of other diversified graphics services. The photocopy scene was still in its infancy and it took a mechanical engineer to properly operate the large, expensive and exceedingly complex machinery involved. Joe did have an engineering degree but it was from a European university. He was a Polish Jew who had survived the Holocaust by moving from country to country and almost literally surviving on his wits. He did not like to talk about his experiences, but occasionally he would let something slip about his horrendous life during the World War II years. Joe was most likely somewhere between 45 and 55 and just slightly overweight. His best features were his steel blue eyes and curly, iron gray hair. His hair was similar to that of my Cantor. In fact, he slightly resembled the Cantor. The big difference was that Joe responded readily to my obvious attraction.

Joe had reason to be in the store on a daily basis both for his company and for his own part time photography business. Since his was a commercial account, he fell under my jurisdiction. It was not long before our conversations began to contain a slight undertone of flirtation. Even I soon began to realize that.

For several months that was where the relationship remained. Then one day Joe invited me to have lunch with him. Then it was lunch several times a week. Soon after that it progressed to a drink after work, before I headed home and he went back to work for what he said would be an hour or two to finish up. That drink became a nearly daily occurrence. I could talk freely with Joe about many things, and I thoroughly enjoyed being with him. I began to have some romantic fantasies about him, but they remained fairly chaste—at least at first. I even thought about inviting him to my parents' home for dinner, but something told me that my friendship with this older man would not meet with approval in spite of his being Jewish.

One day Jay took me aside and asked me what was going on between me and Joe. "You're not seeing him after work, are you?" he asked.

"Just a drink," I replied. "We're not having an affair, if that's what you mean."

Jay looked serious. "I think he's married," he said. "Has he told you that he isn't?"

I had not given it too much thought. Somehow I had always perceived Joe as being too wrapped up in his work and too busy to have any real home life.

"I don't want you to get hurt," Jay continued. "This is a guy who could hurt you if you leave yourself open to it."

At some point, I asked Joe some questions about his personal life that he answered somewhat evasively. The more I asked, the more evasive he became. We were sitting at a little table in the cocktail lounge we favored for our after work libation. Joe suddenly reached for my hand and clasped it between both of his, firmly but gently.

"Let's talk about something else," he said.

"I don't want to talk about anything else," I replied. "I want to talk about you."

He smiled his ingratiating smile. "You know enough about

me," he stated. "Some day I'll tell you more. Right now I just want to be with you. REALLY be with you."

He was still holding my hand, and my heart was beating, it seemed, very loudly. I didn't know what to say, though, so I waited for him to go on.

"Would you like to go to a hotel?" he asked, so quietly and matter-of-factly that it did not shock me. "I know you live with your parents."

I wanted to ask him if he did too, or why we couldn't go to his house. Instead, I became very tongue-tied. I knew the answer. "Joe—are you married?" I asked.

His gaze dropped from my eyes to our entwined hands on the table. "Yes," he admitted and then added what even then sounded like a horrible cliché. "My wife doesn't understand me. Not like you do."

I was on the verge of tears, but I was not about to cry in front of him. Instead, I rose from my chair and turned toward the door, leaving my half finished drink on the table. I tried to say at least good-bye, but the words were caught in my throat. I hurried out of the lounge and walked to the bus stop where I could catch my ride home.

<center>~~~</center>

Among the commercial customers with whom I dealt was a first rate portrait photographer by the name of David Martin. He was quiet, a little shy and very fond of opera and classical music. There was something vaguely mysterious about him. David and I hit it off almost immediately. Although he was not a daily visitor in the store, we managed to talk on the telephone nearly every day. Our conversations ran the gamut of music, motion pictures, current events and trivia as well as photography. He kept telling me about his home and the studio he had built that served also as his living room. I kept asking him when I would be able to see it. I was thoroughly intrigued with Dave. In his late thirties, he was not handsome, but I found him attractive. I looked forward to his coming to the store and to his calls and soon realized that I felt more and more physically drawn to him.

I sometimes threw caution to the winds when I was speaking with Dave. One day he phoned an order in to the store, which I wrote up and then continued to chat with him about several non-related subjects. I was unaware that Jay's mother, who often came into the store purportedly to help out but actually to spy on the employees, was standing nearby and listening to every word I was saying. The other line was ringing, and I fully intended to tell Dave as soon as he finished with what he was telling me that I had to answer it. Before that could occur, Jay's mother moved closer and hovered behind me, reaching around my shoulder to indicate the line that was lit and ringing. I nodded my head, still listening to Dave. The woman would not be put off. She dug her finger in between my shoulder blades and shouted, "Answer the phone!"

I have never tolerated being touched by someone I don't like, and I definitely disliked Jay's meddling mother. Her finger still drilling into my back, I whirled around in my desk chair, put the phone down and grabbed a glass paperweight. She backed off, seeing my anger, and I flung the paperweight in her direction, barely missing her head. She beat a hasty retreat. I picked up the phone and told Dave I would call him later and explain. Then I wrote a quick note to Jay to tell him what I had done in the heat of anger and that I was quitting, since he would be firing me anyway and I wanted to spare him the trouble. I got my purse from my desk drawer, retrieved my coat from the closet in the rear of the store and walked out.

That night Jay called me and asked me to consider coming back. He knew how his mother affected the employees much of the time. There had been several good workers who had quit because of her. He did not want to lose me.

"I lost my temper," I told him. "Badly. It's inexcusable. I could have hurt her if the paperweight had hit her in the head. I think I *wanted* to hurt her. Jay, I think I wanted to *kill* her. I can't stand being touched like that. I went crazy for a minute."

"Who were you talking to when it happened?" he asked.

"Dave Martin."

I heard Jay chuckle. "Why am I not surprised?" he asked. "You really like that guy, don't you?"

"Yes, I do," I replied.

"I'll talk to Mom," said Jay. "I'll ask her to stay home for a few days. It would be better all around if she didn't come in anyway. Will you come back?"

I did.

My relationship with Dave Martin continued. One day he invited me to come for lunch at his studio/home the following Saturday and I was deliriously happy. I couldn't wait for the weekend and that first visit.

I fell in love with Dave's house. It was very masculine, yet it was welcoming and comfortable. Sparsely furnished, the typically small San Francisco rooms appeared much larger than they actually were, due to the openness and lack of clutter. The main room was a combination living room and studio with a highly polished hardwood floor and inviting leather sofa and chairs. A studio view camera on a sturdy tripod occupied a prominent spot with a large pull-down screen opposite it. Flood and spotlights were set up all around, along with stands that held matte silver reflectors. On the back wall were several poster sized portraits of very handsome young men. I recognized one of them as a popular football player.

"This is it," said Dave, smiling his endearing, slightly crooked smile. "What do you think?"

"I love it," I replied. I noticed several portfolios stacked on the large coffee table. I indicated them. "Your photos?" I asked.

He nodded. "Would you like to see them?"

I said that I did.

"Coffee or tea?" he asked. "I think I have Coke too."

I don't remember what I requested, but he left the room and shortly returned with it. Then he picked up the top portfolio and opened it. It contained a series of action sports photographs—very excellently done ones with dramatic lighting and quality printing.

"You do your own printing, don't you?" I asked. "These are really good."

He grinned. "Want to see my darkroom?" he asked.

"Of course."

Dave led me through one of the two doors, down a short hallway and into a room that had undoubtedly been intended to be a guest bedroom. It was a well-designed, neat as a pin and spotlessly clean darkroom. He had the best equipment—Omega enlarger, stainless steel trays, professional print dryer and a large assortment of boxes of photographic paper. Everything was very well organized. There were a few prints thumbtacked to the walls. All of them were well-lighted and composed pictures of young men in various poses. All were shirtless.

"My specialty," Dave answered my unasked question. "Portraits of men."

That was not all he did. I learned that day that Dave's chief source of income was from the sale of very classy male nudes, many of which were ordered from advertisements in magazines and sent through the U.S. Mail, something which, during the 1950's, was still illegal. Dave made quite a bit of money from these—enough to be purchasing the Pacific Heights home and expensive equipment he had. He admitted that he was breaking the law but was quick to explain that he felt the law was unfair and unjust. It was all right to send photos of female nudes through the postal service but to do that with male frontal nudity was considered a felony. I agreed with him right away. It took a little longer for me to fully realize who were his clientele and the inescapable fact that Dave himself was a homosexual.

The H word was never spoken between us, and Dave never admitted to it. We continued for several months to see quite a bit of one another. He had no car, so mostly I would go to his house and he would either make a meal at home or we would go out to a nice nearby restaurant. I thought about Dave all the time and would wonder what he was doing. I called him frequently and he called me almost as often. I was quite sure that I was in love with him, although there was rarely any physical contact between us. When it happened, it was always a comforting arm around my shoulders or a quick but strong hug.

One day Dave called and said that he would be going away for a while. When I asked for details they were not forthcoming. Around the same time I noted that his sizable bill at Carter's had become delinquent. It was my job, since he was my customer, to find out what was going on. When I called him, I learned that his phone had been disconnected. Some of what ensued is no longer too clear in my mind. Possibly it never was; but somehow I found out that Dave had been arrested and found guilty of selling and sending lewd and lascivious photographs through the mail. It evidently was not his first conviction, and he was sentenced to several years in prison, to be served at Terminal Island near Long Beach.

I immediately wrote to him, but the letter was returned, since

I was not on his list of people with whom he could correspond. I was very unhappy and quite desperate. I contacted the authorities, asking to be put on Dave's mail list. They wanted to know if I was family and I came close to lying about that but decided it would be prudent to be truthful. I explained that I was a close friend and that, to the best of my knowledge, Dave had no family to speak of. Eventually someone asked him if he wanted to hear from me and he said yes. I was then able to correspond with him.

Dave was thoroughly depressed and, I was sure, potentially suicidal. Prison life, although he had been given an office job, was hard enough; but he knew that he would lose his house and his studio, not to mention his livelihood. I asked him if there was some way I could take over the payments on his house so he wouldn't lose it. He turned down the offer, most likely feeling that I would expect to live there, which would not be much different from the mortgage being foreclosed. He also did not wish to feel indebted to anyone—not even a good friend. His letters were well-written and heart wrenching. He told me that he could never give me what he knew I wanted and deserved. He compared himself and me and our friendship to the characters in a book by Ayn Rand that we had both read.

Dave was allowed minimal visits from people on his list of contacts, so I arranged to go to see him at Terminal Island. It involved an eight hour Greyhound bus ride each way, but I would have done much more than that to be able to be with him if only for an hour or so. I wound up going to see him once a month for nearly six months. Then he wrote to me that he did not wish to see me anymore, that it was too hard on both of us. I argued with him by mail, but he would not change his stand. He said he would refuse to see me if I came down anyway. The trip was too draining for me to risk that, but I continued to beg him by mail to allow me to visit. He wrote that he did not want to see me waste my time and my life hoping for something that he could never be for me. Shortly after that he began to refuse my letters, and they were returned.

When Dave was due to be released on parole a year or so later, he did contact me to ask me to try to find a low rent apartment for him before he returned to San Francisco. He had lost his house and all of his photo equipment and he had no idea what he would do. I saw him only once after he came back, when I drove him to the small living quarters I had located for him. He was thinner than he had been the last time I had seen him, and his skin was pale and sallow. His graying light brown hair was cut very short. His eyes lacked the sparkle they had usually contained when I had known the old Dave. When I dropped him off at his apartment I elicited a promise from him that he would call me soon. He never did.

CHAPTER TWENTY

ROMANCE, THE REAL THING

During the years I was at Carter's someone was always trying to fix me up with what they felt was the perfect date for me. Jay himself was one of the few people who never made this attempt. He knew me well enough to understand that I would find Mr. Right, if one existed, in due time and I would have to do it on my own.

One of the would-be matchmakers was Bob Landau. He worried about me almost from our first meeting and even more so after the Ponder & Best job fiasco. He was always trying to find a nice Jewish boy for me. One of his attempts was a young New Yorker who was moving to the Bay Area to replace Bob as the local sales representative. Bob was moving to the Los Angeles area for a managerial position with Ponder & Best. Bob said that his replacement was a good looking, well educated and promising fellow who was very concerned about not knowing anyone in his new location.

"He's a little shy, I think," Bob told me. "I thought you might show him around San Francisco." With a twinkle in his eye, he added, "Besides, who knows what might come of it?"

I was less than enthused. My arranged dates had never panned out quite the way their well-meaning originators had intended. I had just broken off with another customer—this one from Pacific Gas & Electric across the street—and was not ready to embark on a new relationship. I had briefly gone out with the sales rep from one of Ponder & Best's rivals and had written that particular one off as a total loss in spite of his jovial manner, expensive car and speed boat, in which I was sure he would one day get himself killed. I had no intention of being with him on that occasion.

The new Ponder & Best salesman duly called on Carter's only a day after his move to San Francisco. He was, as Bob had described, nice looking and charming. He sought me out after having introduced himself to Jay and asked if I had given any thought to showing him around town. I agreed to dinner and a ride around the city the following evening.

All went well until it was, I felt, time to say goodnight. At that point he suggested that we go to my place, since his hotel room was small and ugly. He assured me that he would have something better by our next date but for the time being it would have to be my house. I had a very difficult time convincing him that I did not want to end the evening in bed with him. At first he acted as if he didn't believe me. Then he became insulting and asked if I didn't like men, that Bob hadn't told him that I was a lesbian. Eventually I told him that I lived with my parents and there was no way I could bring a man home with me. I also told him that I didn't know yet whether I liked him well enough to have sex with him. I was, at that point, quite sure that I didn't care for him to that extent. It was a good thing, too, because gossip made the rounds quickly in the photo sales industry. I learned within a day or two that the new Ponder & Best sales representative had a wife and two children still in New York, waiting for him to find a place to live in the San Francisco area before they drove out to join him.

There were other romantic failures in the first ten years of my working life, and I had resigned myself to being single and loveless. I was still dealing with Dave Martin's incarceration and a comfortable but unexciting alliance with a divorced, fifty-ish fellow camera club member when a uniformed sailor came into the store one day to ask about local camera clubs. He had walked along much of Market Street to find a camera shop and had passed several of them before he had walked into Carter's. He was unable to explain why he had bypassed the other stores and had chosen that particular one, but the clerk who waited on him immediately called me, knowing that I was an active member of the California Camera Club. It was one of those instances that often have me convinced that there is such a thing as fate.

The sailor was stationed on an aircraft carrier that had just arrived at the Hunter's Point Naval Shipyard for an extensive overhaul and would be there for several months. I told him about the club, wondering why a sailor would be interested in one and certain that he would never show up at a meeting. I was wrong. He appeared the following Tuesday evening, and I asked him his name so I could introduce him.

"Arthur Barber," he said.

"Do they call you Arthur or Art?" I asked matter-of-factly.

"Don," he replied. Noting the question on my face, he added, "That's my middle name. I'm Arthur Donald Barber, Jr. and I don't want to be a Junior."

For the next several months Don Barber attended every meeting he could attend, which was most of them. He was invited along for our after meeting coffee sessions, which were always much more interesting than the actual club meetings. He was quiet and rarely spoke except when someone asked him about his life in the Navy. Having a member of the military in the club was a bit of an oddity. In June of 1958 Don's ship left for another eight month deployment to the Far East, and our little coffee group went back to what it had been before his arrival.

During the Holidays at the end of the year I received a Christmas card from Don. The brief note that accompanied it said that the ship would be back at Hunter's Point in February. Almost as a post script there was a question. Would I have dinner with him?

I considered for quite some time how I should reply. I had been very unsuccessful with nearly all of my dealings with men. Some of it had been due, I knew only too well, to my innate shyness, naiveté and fear of making a mistake. Much of that came from my early background and the way I had grown up. Some came from simply being involved several times with men who were very wrong for me. Self doubt also crept into the equation. My mother's oft-repeated statements about men not liking women who wore glasses or who were too smart had had more effect on me than I liked to admit. I was not beautiful, not graceful, not talented, not any of the things that would make a woman attractive to a man. On the other hand, I had rarely lacked male companionship, although much of it was not really what I wanted. I was confused, unhappy and a prime candidate for help I did not know how to find.

I could always talk with Jay. Jay was very much aware of my conflicted feelings and of most of the reasons for them. Jay had not seen too much of Don, but he knew about the quiet sailor and was not surprised that I had received a tentative invitation from him. Mostly he was aware of my painfully impossible love for Dave Martin. He told me to accept the dinner invitation. After all, what was there to lose? It could be a distraction if not much else. I knew that he was hoping, for my sake, that it would be much more than that.

February came very quickly. One day a trim Navy Chief Petty Officer appeared in the store. At first I did not recognize Don in his new uniform. He had recently been promoted from Electrician's Mate First Class to the new rating of Nuclear Weaponsman Chief. The suit and tie look of the CPO uniform made him appear older and taller, not to mention more handsome. Once I had absorbed the change in his appearance, and in spite of having known that he would be arriving at some point, I was surprised to actually see him in the store.

"I'm back," he announced. "Is tonight all right?"

I was unprepared and stood silently regarding him.

"Do I look that different?" he asked.

He didn't, really, once I knew who it was. "It's the uniform," I said. "That's different."

"I just made Chief," he ventured. "It's the first time I've worn the dress uniform."

"It looks—good," I said slowly. I didn't really know what to say.

"We're not going to be at Hunter's Point very long this time," said Don. "I'm not quite sure what our schedule will be, but we'll be operating out of Alameda for a while."

That was February of 1959. By the end of March we were seeing each other nearly every evening and on weekends. As different as our backgrounds were—Don and his two years younger brother had been raised by a single mother in New York City—we had a great deal in common besides photography. Don enjoyed classical music, serious motion pictures, books and art in spite of no one else in his family having any of those interests. Although he was a bit of a loner, he was liked by his shipmates. With no money available for higher education, he had spent his entire adult life in the

Navy and was used to being told everything from what to wear to what he was going to eat. That kind of life had suited him and he had advanced quickly through enlisted ranks. He obeyed orders and studied what he needed to study in order to get ahead. He was quite sure that he would eventually retire as a Master Chief with 30 years of service and he told me how secure a future that would mean. I failed to realize that his telling me this was actually a shy form of proposal. It was not until we were having a cup of the suddenly popular cappuccino one night at a North Beach coffee house that we realized the odd looking espresso maker we were discussing was something we both wanted to have in our home—and that home, in the future, was one and the same.

Don was a perfect gentleman. He opened doors for me, carried packages, always asked where I wanted to go before planning an outing and, above all, made no sexual overtures during or at the end of any of our dates. We hugged and kissed and held hands and often wound up parked on Twin Peaks, our arms entwined as we watched the fascinating San Francisco nightscape unfold below us.

In April the Navy sent Don to school in San Diego for several weeks. From the start I missed him. He called a few days after he had left and invited me to come and spend a weekend at his mother's home in Garden Grove. He suggested that we could go to Disneyland if I wanted. I didn't have to think too long about the invitation before accepting.

We spent two days at Disneyland, a visit that culminated in his asking me to marry him, with the wedding to take place after he returned from his carrier's next eight month deployment. They were due to leave in August.

At nearly 28, I had been officially engaged twice previously and had broken off the engagement when I had realized that marriage in that particular situation would have been a disaster. I knew immediately that this time it was very different. I also knew that there were some problems, not the least of which was, although neither Don nor I practiced our religion, that he was a Protestant and I was Jewish. The biggest part of that problem could be our respective families. There was also something else I had never told Don. I did not want children, which was undoubtedly another effect of my less than happy childhood and adolescence. I was very much afraid that would not go over well with him. The third problem was his mother. Although not a mama's boy in the traditional sense of the word, Don had been extremely close to his mother and had been very helpful to her financially. In fact, she had been receiving a sizable allotment from his pay each month. Before the Disneyland weekend was over, his mother had even taken me aside and had begged me not to take her boy away from her, a difficult conversation with which I had a very hard time dealing. I had found that request quite frightening. Then there was the matter of money. The pay of military personnel, even those who had enlisted for a career, in those years was very poor. There were benefits that made up for some of this lack, especially in the matter of retirement. It was not until quite a few years later that the whole structure of remuneration for service members was changed and, in exchange for giving up some of the fringe benefits, the actual pay was increased to be more on a par with the pay scale of civilian workers. Because Don's duty station would probably change at least every four years there was no guarantee that we would be able to remain in the San Francisco Bay Area, which meant that I might have to give up my position. I already knew that Don had assumed quite a bit of financial responsibility for his mother. This was something to think about.

We talked briefly and almost superficially about these potential pitfalls. Don was very reassuring regarding most of them. He could not promise me that there would be no financial obligations toward his mother, but he was certain that things could be worked out. Unlike me, he was not a chronic worrier. When it came to the matter of children, to my huge surprise he concurred. He, too, had little desire to raise a family. He did say that he occasionally had thought about adopting an older child—perhaps one from a minority or from overseas.

"We can decide on that in a few years," he said. "Maybe when we're more settled and know where we're going to be in the future."

I accepted his proposal. Becoming engaged at Disneyland seemed about as close to living out a fairytale as possible.

The Wedding, July 17, 1959

CHAPTER TWENTY ONE

END OF AN ERA

Eventually Don's attempts to obtain duty in the Bay Area succeeded, and after an unhappy year in San Diego, which in the 1960's was more of an overgrown village than the cosmopolitan center it was later to become, we moved back to Northern California. I went back to work at Carter's in the position of assistant manager. I really tried to take up where I had left off, but things were considerably different from the way they had been. The sales manager Jay had hired had not been able to pick up the pieces, and Jay's constant need for more income was not being met. The growing popularity of huge discount stores and chain businesses had been causing ever greater problems for small, family owned companies since they had so much more buying power and could, as a result, sell at lower prices. People still came into places like Carter's, but they came to pick our brains about cameras and other equipment and then would go to one of the big chains to buy at a deeply discounted price that the small store was unable to match. I could sense the desperation Jay felt as sales volume decreased and Carter's dropped increasingly into the red. I also began to be aware that he no longer confided in me as much as he had done in the past. In fact, he often seemed to be evasive and unwilling to get into any kind of discussion with me.

The reason for Jay's changed attitude became clear one day when he came into the store an hour or so later than usual. He was accompanied by a handsome, sharp looking younger man in a "dress for success" business suit. He immediately called a staff meeting and introduced the man as Gerd Filges, the ex-sales manager of German photographic giant Agfa's United States operation and as of that day, Carter's new general manager. This Germanic hotshot had convinced Jay that he could exponentially increase sales and generate a very large amount of money for the business. However, in order to accomplish this, Jay had to give him full power over everything in the store, which included the employees. The only thing he could not do without going to Jay first was to fire either the sales manager or me.

Mr. Filges assumed control of Carter's the next day. He strode through the door that morning and demanded everyone's full attention. He shouted, Hitler style, every word distinctly as he told us he was in command and that he expected full cooperation.

"I do not expect you to like me," he said in his heavy German accent. "You will do as I say and do nothing without my permission. Anyone who does not follow this instruction can pack up all his or her personal things and leave. Don't ever bother to say good morning to me or to ask me how I am. You don't care how I am and I don't care how *you* are, or if you have a good morning or not. You will merely obey. Do you all understand?"

There was a shocked silence, and before the end of the day the sales manager had given notice that he was quitting. Mr. Filges informed me, still in a raised voice but not quite as loudly as he had addressed the entire staff, that I was not to expect to become the sales manager. He did not believe in women in managerial positions.

"Your duties will be cashier and some office work," he told me. "There will be an adjustment to your salary, of course, because you will no longer have so many responsibilities. I will deal with the professional customers myself. You will have nothing further to do with them. Understood?"

Within a few days the entire atmosphere at Carter's had become funereal. Jay had been asked to not come to the store at least until the new regime was well in place and operating smoothly. Everyone hated coming to work in the mornings and we labored through the days with the greatest of difficulty, using more of our energies to avoid confrontation with the despised new manager than we did for performing our tasks. I frequently had to resist the temptation of replying to Gerd Filges' orders with a "Heil Hitler" salute. I had also begun to get up each morning with a sour stomach and a near need to vomit. Mr. Filges had arrived a few days before the Fourth of July weekend, and I realized on the morning of the Fourth, when I didn't have to go to work, that my recently chronic intestinal upset had gone on hiatus. I realized then for certain that my illness had been brought on by the change in my work situation, and it did not take me long to make up my mind to submit my resignation despite the fact that quitting my job would probably mean a need for a total change of lifestyle. Other than my nearly 14 years at Carter's I had worked only a short time for a camera shop in San Diego while Don had briefly been stationed in that area, at Camp Elliot. I had not enjoyed being "one of the girls" in the store. Other than that, I had no real work experience. Besides, in the years since my high school graduation, a college degree had become increasingly important and usually necessary for obtaining meaningful employment, whether or not the job itself really required one. I didn't have one. However, I had, over the years, built up a viable ability to utilize the resources I did have. One of them was my connection with various sales representatives from the wholesalers with whom I had dealt on behalf of Carter's. One of them was the Eastman Kodak salesman. In those days Eastman Kodak was still the major player in the photographic field and the first name that would come to mind when thinking of any form of picture taking or the equipment and accessories for doing it.

I had the Kodak representative's home phone number and, in spite of my reluctance to bother him during his time off, I called him. He knew of the change in Carter's management and had already experienced Gerd Filges' demeaning behavior, which extended to the employees of Carter's' suppliers as well as our own. My call did not come as a complete surprise.

"I can't stay there," I told him. "I've been waking up sick to my stomach every morning, knowing I have to go to work in that place."

I could almost see the Kodak rep's smile over the phone. "Well, we can't have that. I'll see what I can do," he told me. "Give me your home phone number so I don't have to call you at the store."

Without waiting for any job news from the Kodak salesman I requested a meeting with Mr. Filges as soon as I arrived at work on Monday morning. He called for me almost immediately. Unlike

Jay, who had his desk just behind the doorway that led from the store to the photo studio, Filges had set up a desk on the mezzanine, where he could look down over the balcony railing and observe what was going on throughout the entire sales area below.

Somehow my natural shyness had disappeared by the time I mounted the stairs to the mezzanine. Although my heart was pounding, I walked stolidly up to Filges and, without any meaningless preliminaries, stated flatly that I was giving him notice. "I'll stay the obligatory two weeks if you want," I said. "But I'll leave right now if you'd rather."

I was surprised at his very pleasant smile and handshake. It was several days before I realized that my quitting was exactly what he had wanted, since he had agreed not to fire me. He did ask me to stay for two weeks so I could turn my records and whatever else I knew about the professional part of the business over to him. He needed to pick my brains. For the duration of my stay at Carter's Gerd Filges was very nice to me. At some point during my last day he invited me to have dinner with him at Fishermen's Wharf that night. I was not particularly anxious to go, but I accepted. A farewell dinner at the company's expense was at least a way to say goodbye to the years that had done a great deal to shape the rest of my life. The dinner turned out to be enjoyable, with very little shoptalk and no unpleasantness whatsoever. Gerd Filges had a certain amount of polish and charm when he wanted to turn it on, and I began to understand how he could have convinced Jay to do what he had done.

I heard from the Eastman Kodak salesman within a few days. He had learned that Technicolor was looking for someone for their customer service department. I also had a call from Bob, a young man who did some of the darkroom work for Carter's as well as pickups and deliveries. Bob was a sweet, open and uncomplicated boy with minimal skills and an incomplete high school education. He had worked at Carter's for several years before being drafted into the Army. He was obviously fond of me and, although he was several years younger, I had gone out with him several times before I was married. I understood his strengths and limitations and had managed to get the best out of him as an employee. When he came back after his military service in Alaska Bob had a wife and five children, which included a set of twins and one or two offspring from his wife's first marriage.

Bob was desperately unhappy. He was as upset with having to work under the Filges regime as I had been. He wanted to quit Carter's, especially since I had left; but with a large family to support, not even a high school diploma and no job leads, there was no way out for him.

"Do you have a job yet?" he asked me. "Can you help me find one?"

I hadn't even started at Technicolor yet. I considered Bob's limited education and abilities. He was very likable and he was an excellent driver, so I thought maybe Eastman Kodak might have use for him in their warehouse. I called the Kodak rep again and sure enough, he arranged an interview for Bob.

A week later I went to Carter's to pick up some film I had left for developing and printing while I had still been employed there. Bob had been hired by Kodak and had already left. Gerd Filges evidently saw me from his mezzanine lookout and buzzed the sales floor to tell them that he wanted to see me.

The Gerd Filges who confronted me from the other side of his desk was the same maniacal tyrant who had walked into Carter's and shouted instructions on his first day there. His face was livid as he glared at me.

"You are no longer to speak to any of the employees," he shouted. "You are not wanted in the store. Get out and stay out. No phone calls with employees. Do you understand?"

I knew immediately that this was about Bob, who had undoubtedly blurted out the fact that I had helped him to find another job.

"If you ever set foot in this store again I will have you thrown out," Filges continued, his rage increasing. "I mean it."

Briefly I hovered between wanting to turn and run and to face him squarely and tell him that my personal friendships had nothing to do with Carter's Photo Supply, nor could he impinge on my freedom of speech. I felt the blood flooding into my brain and for the moment was unable to think clearly. My lips trembled in an attempt to come up with something incisive to say. I turned and headed for the stairs, but something made me stop and turn around after taking only a few steps down. At that point I uttered words I had never before and rarely since then said publicly.

"Mr. Filges," I addressed him almost calmly. "Go fuck yourself". With that I walked down the stairs and out of the store for the last time.

CHAPTER TWENTY TWO

WORKPLACE MEMORIES

My career at Technicolor was not especially spectacular, but many things happened during those twelve years that further shaped the direction of my life. It was my first experience in the corporate world, for one thing, and much of that experience was an eye opener.

During my first few years at Technicolor I occasionally met Jay from Carter's Photo Supply for dinner. Things were not going well for Carter's in spite of Gerd Filges' promise to make the business profitable. It was not entirely Filges' fault, though. For one thing, there were monumental changes to the downtown area of San Francisco, and the foot of Market Street experienced a resurgence that included tearing down many of the old buildings to construct newer, taller ones on their sites. Included in the change was the building in which Carter's had been operating for so many years. For some reason both Jay and Gerd Filges had failed to plan adequately for that possibility, which at the last minute before they were forced to vacate sent them scrambling madly for new quarters for the store. Quite a few businesses in that part of town had the same idea, with adequate and affordable quarters very much at a premium. Not wanting to lose the customer base that had been built up over the years, they wanted to remain close by. Eventually they did find a nearby location but at a rental that was so high that operating profitably became an impossibility. Carter's collapsed and filed for bankruptcy within a short time after their move, and I no longer had the opportunity to see Jay. I don't know what he did for income after that. I was extremely saddened when I learned not too long afterwards that he had gone into a diabetic coma and succumbed to his disease. I wept for Jay as if he had been a member of my family. In a way he had been. He certainly had played a very incisive role in my passage into adulthood.

The first eye popping experience was when I realized that the person in charge of the entire customer service department, the sales manager, was much more inclined to party than to work and had been getting away with it for years. He was very good at delegating projects, and upper management did not seem to care how he spent his own working hours as long as everything got done. He was amiable and laid back about most things and would often hang out in the customer service office rather than in the sales office next door. He and the head of customer service, a slim, attractive and very driven woman by the name of Toni Mountain (she was small and extremely un-mountainlike), would talk animatedly for hours.

Toni was a perfectionist and a tough taskmistress. She worked long hours and more than made up for the time spent yakking with the sales manager. She often admitted to having worked until 10 or 11pm the night before in spite of having a family at home more than an hour's commute away. I realized within a few weeks that part of the reason Toni chose to remain at work so many hours was that things were not going too well for her at home.

Things were not going well at Technicolor either. The consumer products division, which consisted of wholesale film and photofinishing services, was a subsidiary of Technicolor in Hollywood. The San Francisco plant was one of four in California with Sacramento and Fresno falling under the same management. The Hollywood consumer products plant had its own offices and its own sales, billing and customer service departments. The San Francisco division had recently moved into an entirely new and much larger facility, had acquired the latest in processing equipment and was trying very hard to compete against the firmly established Eastman Kodak processing plant in Palo Alto. Handicapped by the high cost of doing business in San Francisco, Technicolor had an unending battle with a very strong union—something with which Kodak, only about 30 miles away, had no problem.

The sales department worked very hard to wrap up contracts

with hundreds of drug stores and camera shops in the entire Bay Area. During the changeover to the new factory and new machinery and ever increasing workload there often were processing accidents, which meant quite a bit of work for the customer service department. The worst of these were the twin-check disasters. In those days customers' films were identified by numbered stickers—identical numbers on the finishing envelope and on the end of the roll of film. Later this numbering would be done photographically; but while the stickers were in use it was not uncommon for these to fall off a number of films while they were in one of the processing solutions. When that happened it meant that some customers would receive the wrong pictures. All too frequently a rack of film would fall off its hangers and wind up in the bottom of the developing tank. Not only were some of the negatives scratched but identifying the correct envelopes for the tangle of a dozen or more films became a major project for customer service. This was bad enough in the case of still photos, but when it happened with 8mm movie film, it became a complete nightmare.

Part of customer service's job was to look at these stray films and make notes regarding their contents, then to contact the individual customers in an attempt to find out which roll belonged to whom. The department head's job was to make sure the six of us working in the office were doing our jobs—and to be the final barrier between an angry customer and a potential lawsuit. Toni often had customers come into the office to look at pictures in an attempt to find which belonged to them. She seemed to enjoy talking with these people and spent a great deal of time doing so. Meanwhile other parts of her job remained not done, giving her an excuse to work overtime. We had a myriad other duties—from expediting a suddenly needed order that had to be located somewhere in the plant to writing clear instructions and following through on returned work that, for one reason or another, had to be done over.

I learned quickly that Toni was also coming in to work on Saturdays and occasionally on Sundays as well. There were many things she did not trust any of the rest of us to do properly, so she would pile up work on her desk to do herself. I liked Toni and wanted to help, but the more I tried to take on some of the projects on her desk the more she rejected my attempts. The others were just as happy to sit and twiddle their thumbs while letting Toni do all the work. I admired Toni's way with customers and the organized manner in which she could handle business when she was inclined to do so. When she was in the mood to chat, she was an interesting, stimulating and knowledgeable conversationalist.

One day I noticed that Toni was taking quite a few pills and I casually asked her if something was wrong.

"I'm all right," she replied unconvincingly. "I just have a headache".

I soon learned that Toni's headaches were potential killers. One day when I insisted on staying over to help her with a particularly bad film mix-up she told me that she had an aneurysm in the back of her neck and it sometimes gave her a nearly unbearable migraine. I understood immediately. It was just like the problem my one time boyfriend, Dick Shankel, had. Very much like Dick, Toni was very reluctant to admit any kind of weakness and would drive herself much harder than necessary to disguise the situation. I told Toni about Dick and from that point on she allowed me to be considerably more helpful. Don was overseas at that point in time and I started to spend some time working with Toni after hours. We sometimes went to dinner together, and I was really beginning to enjoy our friendship.

As my one year mark with Technicolor approached, Toni asked me when I was planning to take my vacation. She had some days marked off for herself and wanted me to go before then so I would be back and could cover for her while she was gone. When I was leaving the office on my last day of work the sales manager came up behind me and asked me if I had a minute. It was the first time he had spoken to me directly other than a perfunctory greeting from time to time when we had encountered one another somewhere in the plant.

"Yes, of course," I replied.

"Let's go into my office," he said.

I had no idea what he could want from me, but I followed him.

"You probably think I have no idea what's going on," he told me. "I'm a lot sharper than most people think." His demeanor was very serious, which, in his case, was rare. "I'm going to ask you something and I want a truthful answer," he said.

I was becoming increasingly puzzled as well as more nervous.

"Do you think you could do Toni's job?"

The question was like a sudden clap of thunder and just as unexpected. I'm not sure what kind of expression I had on my face as I thought about this and tried to formulate a reply.

"I think you can," he went on. "I've been watching you". He went on to explain that Toni had started out really well but that her job performance had been going steadily downhill.

There was much more to it than that. I was sure of it then and I still am now.

"Well?" he asked. "There would be an increase in salary, of course—and being in management means you get parking privileges. What about it?"

The ramifications started to whirl through my head. This would mean that Toni would be fired, no doubt. I didn't really want that to happen. On the other hand, I was certain that it would happen even if I didn't accept the promotion. In fact, he detailed that to me.

"Yes," I said finally, "I think I can do the job."

So, when I returned from my vacation I came back as head of customer service. Toni was gone, and I had a management position that I held until the San Francisco plant was closed eleven years later. Looking back on those years I can't help but think that, for someone with my background and my psyche, it was quite an accomplishment.

CHAPTER TWENTY THREE

JUNE

I KNOW I MUST have been a really late bloomer. In looking over my papers and notes from years ago I came across quite a bit of writing that would attest to this. For instance, the June to whom I refer in the following short poem, written at some point in the mid 1960's, was my closest friend between 1966 and 1975. This friendship was a stormy relationship I had with a strong and unique personality, a relationship that taught me many things about a variety of subjects about the world in general and, as usual, also about myself. The friendship did not end in 1975, but my husband and I moved from the Bay Area, my outlook on the world at large forever changed—mostly for the better. Many business and personal associations contributed to that change, and there is no way I can mention all of them in this collection; but June Hunt is one that I could not possibly leave out.

To June

You, my flamboyant friend,
Are the peacock feather in my cap.
You are my courage,
My place on the map.

You are my sparkle,
My one bit of flash.
You are my swagger,
My color, my dash.

> You are my facade
> And my main claim to fame.
> You bring me to life
> When I just say your name.
>
> With you in my thoughts
> Or, joy, by my side,
> Anonymity is gone,
> And I walk with pride.

❧❦❧

One of the really dyed-in-the-wool dog people I met early in my involvement with purebred dogs was June Hunt. I am willing to bet that June Hunt probably knew more about dogs and the mystique that surrounds the dog show world than just about any other individual I've ever known. She had a genuine and instinctive eye for dogs and, I'm sure, for horses as well; but since I know very little about equines I am unable to completely attest to that. She had at one time been a rodeo barrel racer. Had circumstances been amenable to it, June could have been one of those great all-breed judges that eventually manage to become legendary. She also happened to be one of the dog world's genuine one of a kind characters. Had it not been for June my first show dog might have also been my last. June slowly but surely helped to clarify the sometimes puzzling and private dog show scene for me and sparked in me a certain fascination as well as an enduring love/hate relationship with the dog sport. It took me several years to realize that what once appeared to me to be her attempts to drive me out of the often frustrating dog game may have actually been her way of making sure that I was sufficiently devoted to it (not to mention tough enough) to remain in it!

I first met June Hunt shortly after we had bred our very first Italian Greyhound litter from our first Italian Greyhound bitch, a mediocre but pleasant specimen that was also our first purebred dog of any breed. Since we had acquired Tina from a breeder nearly 500 miles away, we had been left pretty much on our own; but bumbling though we might have been, we found our way to a puppy match and managed to sign up the three puppies that had resulted from our first try at breeding. June was attending the match with Jimmie Clausen, in the 1960's a very active and well-known Northern California breeder of Poodles and Italian Greyhounds. June had with her an absolutely gorgeous nine-month-old male Italian Greyhound that had been given to her. I learned quickly that June was the kind of person who had many and varied things given to her, ranging from a show quality puppy of nearly any breed she wanted, jewelry and various cars and RV's to a broken nose.

We had encountered Jimmie Clausen during the early days of our search for an Italian Greyhound puppy, and we recognized him standing at ringside at the match. As green and novice as I was about dogs and showing, I had, in my usual style, done my homework regarding the breed and could see the obvious quality in the striking dog held by Jimmie's companion. I also noticed that the attractive middle-aged woman with the dog had an incredible and enviable aplomb that was readily apparent from the way she stood and moved and, in general, handled herself.

I greeted Jimmie and indicated the three blue puppies in the exercise pen beside us. "Here they are," I said. "What do you think of them?"

It was June and not Jimmie who answered me. "They're blue puppies," she said, a little disdainfully. June was always disdainful of novices until they had proven their mettle, but at that point, of course, I did not know her and assumed that the deprecation was intended for the puppies—or for me.

"This is June Hunt," Jimmie introduced her. "I'm sorry, but I can't remember your name."

I introduced Don and myself, certain that neither of them would remember either of us nor our names for very long.

June was exactly ten years older than I. She nearly always had a stylish, professional hairdo and well made up features. Years earlier she had helped out a young hairdresser who was down on his luck and he had continued to repay her by freely providing her with the best of his services at no charge. Much of the time she exuded a dancer's rhythm and grace of movement, providing she had not had too much to drink.

Even at the puppy match June showed herself to be an expert dog handler, if somewhat overly theatrical in the manner in which she presented her dogs. She showed her male and one of Jimmie's bitch puppies, taking Best of Breed with her dog and Best of Opposite Sex with Jimmie's puppy. Our three little boys, although they had been faithfully trained to stand on the kitchen counter and to walk on a lead, albeit somewhat haltingly, made complete fools of Don and me as we tried valiantly to show them. We had already learned that there is much more to showing dogs than a sprightly trot around the ring.

"Are you going to stay for the group and root for Nero?" June asked after the breed judging. She had a way of talking without removing the cigarette from her mouth that, for some strange reason, I had always admired in anyone able to manage it. "Maybe you can pick up some pointers on handling."

"What did I do wrong?" I asked.

"It would be easier and shorter to tell you what you did right," replied June, inserting the first of many needles that served to convince me that I could do nothing but make a mess of presenting my dogs.

It was several years later before I realized that June's greatest joy in life was to take a dog into the ring and that even at this early point in our friendship she was promoting my insecurity in order to convince me to let her handle my dogs for me. It was a way for her to get to dogs shows while having someone else pay her expenses.

Although we were as opposite from one another as gravel and cotton balls, the attraction between us was instantaneous and strong, as was the ensuing friendship. History has now seen Damon and Pythias, Laurel and Hardy, Abbott and Costello, the Odd Couple—and June and Lilian. For years June and I went to dog shows and traveled on circuits together. June dog sat for us when Don and I went on several vacations. When I had to have a hysterectomy while Don's Navy career sent him to the Orient, June took care of our dogs until I was able to resume doing so myself. When June needed help with a financial problem, I helped. In our respective ways, we were always there for one another.

I was very much impressed with June's vast knowledge of dogs of all breeds. She kept huge scrapbooks containing pictures cut from magazines of top winning dogs she admired. She had an encyclopedic memory for facts and figures and, above all, an eye for dogs that could be compared with absolute pitch in a musician. In by-passing June, the dog fancy missed out on the opportunity to have a fabulous all-breed judge. Whether June did not consider becoming a judge because she loved exhibiting too much or whether the actual reason was something more personal no one will ever know. She rarely judged even at fun matches. I suspect much of it had to do with the drinking problem she fought most of her life. I think people were afraid to ask her to judge for fear of her having been drinking too much when she showed up for her assignment, if she were to show up at all. I like to think that I knew June better than that. I am almost certain that an opportunity to judge dogs would have meant too much to June for her to allow liquor to interfere. Unfortunately, that sort of respect did not extend to many other activities.

June's attractiveness to men had also contributed to her downfall. Married and divorced six times, she had, at the time I met her, two serious gentleman friends. One of them adored her, spent nearly his entire salary on gifts for her, did everything for her—and was completely repelled by her devotion to the dog fancy. The other, a handsome, debonair alcoholic by the name of Ben, treated June like dirt. He was the one she loved passionately, of course. Many others pursued her, gave her drinks and bought her gifts. June was, especially when she had been drinking, a shameless cock-tease, and the result was often catastrophic. I became accustomed to picking up the pieces.

For quite a few years June was forced to cope with her twin brother, a schizophrenic ex-alcoholic who shared a house with her. A deathbed promise to their mother that she would take care of Stanley had given June the inheritance of an increasingly run-down two-story home in a nice area of Oakland. She worked for a mortgage company and Stan kept house for her, after a fashion. Periodically Stan would wander off and go into a bank or auto dealership and insist that he owned both the Bank of America and Standard Oil and that "they" were after him and wanted to do away with him so they could get his money. Usually that meant he would be picked up by the police and June would have to go to bail him out. Since he was not violent in any way, under the State of California system she was unable to get much public help for him and never had the kind of income that could cover private psychiatric treatment. This situation went on as long as I knew June. Visiting her was often a little like a trip to the Twilight Zone, as Stanley always used to remember people (even if he had never seen them before) as someone from one of his past lives and would spin a lengthy tale about his involvement with them in years long past. These stories could become interactive if one played along and answered him with a few imaginative comments. Actually, there were times when I rather enjoyed creating a fantasy past for myself in which Stanley and I were members of the San Francisco Opera chorus or worked at the Bay Area's classy music store, Sherman, Clay & Co. He and I held these conversations frequently. Once, when June had started a new job and hesitated to ask for time off to go to court with her brother, I went with him to plead his case—something that, until then, I would never have dreamed of doing.

June had been and had done quite a few things that most people would never consider doing. Some of these were things of which she was not proud. Few people knew her complete history, but over the years that we were close I became privy to much of it. For instance, she had at one time worked for the famous (and notorious) Sally Stanford. She had also, for years, been addicted to heroin. While many people would have looked down on her if they had known that fact, I admired her because she had, with little help, kicked the habit. She told me the story of her addiction, which included a brief and stormy marriage to a drugged out black musician, following which she had gone into prostitution in order to maintain her heroin habit. One day, she told me, she had looked into a mirror and had seen what she had become. She had gathered up her remaining heroin and flushed it down the toilet. Then she had packed up some clothes, got into her car and had driven to the heavily wooded Oregon lumber country, as far from large cities and a possible supply of drugs as she could go. She did not go into great detail in describing the horrors of withdrawal, but she did mention that she had gone into a small town drug store and had explained her situation to the sympathetic pharmacist, who gave her some sedatives to help her through the worst of it. Lacking any of the usual marketable skills women needed to make a living, June had persuaded the foreman of the local lumber mill to hire her as a log handler, a job she held for several years while living a reclusive life in an old forest cabin. During those years June's only recreation centered around a saloon frequented by ranchers and lumberjacks. There she had met her next husband, a heavy drinker and a violent man who had repeatedly threatened to kill her, eventually shooting off part of June's left index finger in the final argument before she left him and filed for divorce. After that she had moved back to Oakland, having received a letter from her mother telling her that Stanley had had a breakdown and help was needed with his care.

I always admired June for having been able to overcome her heroin addiction without the assistance the drug users of a few years later were able to receive. I could even overlook that she had replaced heroin with alcohol, and, years later, when a mutual acquaintance referred to June as "dirt", I became absolutely furious in her defense.

My friendship with June had its considerable ups and downs, especially at times when she was drinking heavily. I recall, in particular, one frenetic incident during our association. We had been to a puppy match in Marin County. For some reason that I do not remember we had gone there in my motorhome and stayed overnight, although it was less than a two-hour drive from home. On the way to the match June reminded me of a middle aged couple from that area who had taken us out to dinner on a previous dog show weekend and that we owed these people a dinner. Not being particularly flush at the time, I asked June where she had in mind taking them. June never had any money to spare, and I knew that it would be up to me to subsidize her part of the outing. She said that she knew of a lovely restaurant not too far from the match site where dinner would be moderately priced.

After the match, also for a reason I do not recall, but it probably involved an argument, something that had been occurring with increasing frequency, June and I traded partners. She was to ride to the restaurant with the husband and the wife would ride with me in the motorhome. Although we had left the match at approximately the same time, I arrived at the restaurant at least 45 minutes ahead of June. Two additional people who were joining us for dinner arrived at about the same time I did. We waited in the foyer, and I began to have some misgivings about the outing. Sure enough, when they finally arrived June was already quite intoxicated and her escort was having a difficult time with her. June always wanted to do the driving, and the more she drank the better a driver she considered herself to be. Most of the time she was right, but sometimes she decidedly was not.

The six of us were finally seated at a long table and given menus. It did not take me long to realize that the prices June had quoted to me earlier were about half of the cost of the lowest priced entree that was offered. The money I had in my wallet would not cover a dinner for me plus a part of the cost of our guest couple's dinners. June was seated across the table and two seats over. I tried to attract her attention to the menu, but she was obviously too far gone. In fact, having been unable to find her own glasses, she had reached behind her and grabbed a pair from the nose of a woman, a complete stranger, seated at the next table. I decided that the prudent thing to do would be to order a tuna sandwich and a glass of water for myself rather than a dinner, and maybe I would have enough money to cover June's and my part of the outing.

When everyone else at the table was served a bowl of soup, June asked, "Where's yours?"

"I'm not having any," I replied. "I'm just going to have a tuna sandwich."

"A tuna sandwich!" June exploded. "For *dinner*?"

"I happen to like tuna sandwiches."

"Oh, come off it," June yelled. "You're just being a cheap Jew again."

There was a rather shocked silence around the table. I knew for a fact that at least one of the others, Russ Herman, who was sitting opposite me, was also Jewish. I was very embarrassed.

"Order some real food," June insisted. "I'll pay for it." Then she proceeded to vomit into her soup bowl.

The evening ended with several of the men carrying June, who had fallen asleep at the table with her face in her plate, out to the motorhome. That was the easy part. I had to try to wake her and get her up the flight of outside steps by myself when we reached her house. I avoided weekend dog show trips with June for quite a while after that.

Another incident I remember all too vividly involved Dallas Reichstein, another unforgettable character from the dog world. Dallas was a bartender in one of San Francisco's better known gay bars, a place where June and I had occasionally gone for a drink and an exchange of dog talk. One night around one in the morning Dallas called me at home. He said that my friend June was in the bar, very drunk and disorderly and was I going to come and get her or should he call the police. Of course I immediately put my clothes on and drove there.

That was the easy part. June, in her usual uninhibited manner, was making sexual overtures to several of the bar's customers, none of whom, of course, had any interest whatsoever in her attentions. Dallas told me that June had evidently begun the evening with a date that had subsequently walked out on her when he had discovered what an unpleasant drunk she could be. June had then driven her car into and over some barriers on a street that was closed for construction, doing enough damage to her vehicle that she had been forced to leave it and to continue on foot. By the time she had reached the waterfront locale where she knew that Dallas tended bar she had already entered a most disorderly stage of inebriation. Dallas had asked her to leave, and she had refused, eventually telling him that her car was not running. That was when he had called me.

Dallas, a strapping, handsome man who evidently was a bit of a legend among San Francisco's gay populace, helped me to get a vehemently protesting June into my Karmann Ghia. She said she did not want to leave the bar, and she especially did not want to be taken to my house.

"You don't have much choice," I said. "I'm certainly not going to take you all the way to Oakland at this hour. You'll be fine until morning."

After uttering a number of obscenities June waited for me to stop at a light and got out of the car. I had no alternative but to go after her.

The streets were nearly deserted, but I could not leave June staggering around in the dark. She would either be hit by a car or she would be picked up by the police. After chasing her for nearly half a block I caught up to her and grabbed her by the arm. Somehow I got her back to the car and shoved her in. This time I locked the door from the outside.

Don was waiting up when we got home and helped to get June into the guest bedroom. However, we had no sooner begun to get ourselves back to bed when we heard the door down the hall opening and closing again. June insisted that she was going to go home, that she would walk the 20 or so miles, including the San Francisco-Oakland Bay Bridge crossing, and that we could not keep her against her will. Exasperated, I said I would drive her to Oakland; and I did.

One year when June and I drove to Oregon for the once popular Cal-Ore circuit, a series of five dog shows that annually attracted many dyed-in-the-wool show aficionados, I learned another of June's secrets. She and I traveled in the Volkswagen camper Don and I owned before expanding to a larger motorhome later in our dog show involvement. The VW was comfortable enough for June and me and the two dogs we had with us as far as riding and sleeping; but it had no bathroom facilities. We were able to use the toilets at the various show sites, but in order to shower we had to impose on friends who were staying in motel rooms. This particular year Dallas Reichstein was also on the circuit and June asked him if we could shower at his motel. I noticed some reluctance on Dallas' part, but he said it would be all right. He even came to pick us up at the show site so we wouldn't have to move the camper. I was glad there would be no driving involved because June had already been drinking with several people she knew who were camped on the grounds.

I took my shower first and when I came out June was holding a drink and already looked pretty wasted. Dallas took her glass and persuaded her to go into the bathroom. He told me that he was expecting someone and was hoping to be able to take us back to the show grounds before his company arrived. We listened for the shower, both of us very much aware of June's proclivity for procrastination.

When June emerged from the bathroom she had a towel wrapped around herself but was otherwise stark naked. She strode over to the television set and found some music. She turned up the volume to a definitely louder than motel room level and whirled around, whipping the towel from around her waist and waving it matador style as she began to dance. Then she twirled it as she increased the intensity of her gyrations.

The expression on Dallas' face went from astonishment to annoyance. "Put some clothes on," he ordered.

June ignored his request without missing a beat.

"For God's sake, June," Dallas went on. "Have some respect. If not for yourself then have it for Lilian."

The incident ended with Dallas physically throwing June into the bathroom and closing the door. He apologized to me.

I was completely nonplused. I knew that June had a tendency to drink too much and could become difficult at such times, but this was something I had never experienced—had never even considered. Surely June knew that Dallas was gay. It did not enter my mind that the bizarre performance could possibly have been aimed at me.

June was fond of throwing lavish dinner parties. Both she and her brother were expert gourmet cooks; but most often she directed the event from her spot on the sofa and Stanley did all the work. The food was fabulous and plentiful, but often it was not ready to be served until the wee, small hours of morning. By that time most of the guests had left, and June had tasted too much of the cooking wine.

Christmas at June's house was always a special occasion. There were literally dozens of packages—most of them for her. Most were from her would-be boyfriend, the reclusive, sometimes angry truck driver she preferred, for some obscure reason, to call Joe although his name was Ed. Joe/Ed adored June and courted her for years to no avail, although eventually he became husband #7, mostly for tax and insurance reasons. To the best of my knowledge they never had a real marriage. Joe was always jealous of June's popularity and hated all of her friends, male and female, including me. I don't know if his anger management issues were completely due to June or came from some other source. One year during the traditional Christmas dinner affair both Joe and Ben turned up and in the resulting melee one of them pushed the other down a flight of stairs. June was asleep on the sofa at the time and failed even to wake up.

After several years my devotion to the sport of dogs seemed to be going nowhere. June showed and finished our first four champions while I learned a great deal from her. I supplied the transportation, although she always drove, insisting that she was the only woman in the world who could properly drive a motorhome—or even a car. It was easier to allow her to take the wheel than to argue, especially when she had had a few drinks. I paid the entry fees and other show expenses—and usually provided the muscle to haul crates and exercise pens around. Everyone at the shows knew June and she knew them. She was always off talking with someone while I did the setting up or taking down. It was years before I realized that no one in the dog world actually knew me and, if things didn't change, no one ever would. People would greet me at a dog show not with, "Hello, Lilian!" but with, "Where's June?"

As such things are prone to happen, one day I saw the light—or I thought I did. June had done a fantastic job of convincing me that I was too clumsy to ever be a decent handler. After that moment of illumination my immediate efforts to get away from June's influence and to make it on my own as a "dog person" were nearly as traumatic as a divorce. June proceeded to make me feel guilty whenever I wanted to do something by myself and without her control. I tried hiring a professional handler, the late Evonne Chashoudian, to show for me. Evonne saw my situation and eventually helped me to see it myself. I finally had a dog that showed well for me and I started to enjoy going into the ring. June tried every trick in the book to discourage me, finally accusing me of breaking my promise to let her show my dogs.

Shortly after that Don and I made our move to Southern California, a move dictated by his retirement from the Navy and my being "downsized" from my position with Technicolor. The pre-Proposition 13 property taxes ran out of control. We simply could no longer afford to live in the Bay Area.

With me gone, June switched from Italian Greyhounds and Miniature Pinschers to Japanese Chins and became fairly successful and well known in that breed. I made several trips a year back to Northern California either for dog shows or just to visit. June still continued to accuse me of breaking my promise to her and, although I stayed at her house a few times, the visits were somewhat strained. Periodically she was sober and things were better, but then she would start to drink again and it became the same old story.

On one of my Bay Area visits, in 1991, I was staying at June's house for a few days prior to a judging assignment I had nearby when Don called me there to tell me that my mother had passed away. It had not been completely unexpected, as she had suffered a series of strokes over the past 14 years, each leaving her increasingly incapacitated. The frequency of these incidents had increased dramatically in the preceding few months.

My mother had purchased a burial plot in the Jewish cemetery in Colma beside that of my father, who had died 28 years earlier. When she had suffered her first disastrous stroke in the late 1970's we had moved her, after her release from the hospital and very much against her will, to Southern California where she would be close enough for us to be able to help her if necessary. At first she had lived in a hotel-like assisted living facility that she seemed to enjoy, but when her next stroke left her confined to a wheelchair it had become necessary to move her to a nursing home. We had finally found a decent one in Palm Springs, which was within a few minutes' drive from Morongo Valley, where Don and I were living. Arrangements had been in place for several years for transporting my mother's body, after her death, the approximately 500 miles to the cemetery in Colma. Some phone calls were made, and it was set up for the transport and burial to take place that Thursday.

The only living relatives my mother had in the area were my two cousins in San Francisco and I called them right away. Marianne, the younger one, was away on a trip to visit one of her grown children. Her sister, Lotte, expressed her sympathy but had some reason for not being able to be there for the burial. I had planned to ask one of them to contact a rabbi about a brief graveside ceremony, but when Lotte said she could not be there I decided against it. My mother had not set foot in a synagogue in years and had even attended some Christian prayer services in the nursing home. My own agnosticism came to the fore, and I decided to consider a memorial service at a later date instead. One was actually held a few months later, and it was a very nice one.

I asked June if she would go with me to the cemetery on Thursday. At first she said that she would, but a few minutes later she said she had changed her mind. I really wanted her to go, but she steadfastly refused. I don't think I have ever forgiven her for that.

I drove to Colma by myself fairly early on Thursday and discussed details with the person in charge of the cemetery. I got directions and found my father's headstone and the prepared space next to it. I don't remember much of that day very clearly, but I can still see myself standing, very much alone, by the open grave, waiting for the hearse to arrive, then watching the two quiet men silently lift the coffin into its final resting place and then covering it with its blanket of dirt. After they had gone I remained standing there and mentally saying what I remembered of the Kaddish, the Hebrew prayer for the dead.

After my mother's death I started to become more active in the Southern California dog scene and the trips to the Bay Area became fewer and further between. I saw June only at dog shows, where we exchanged a few pleasantries and promises to "get together" that never happened. Eventually I attended a few shows in her area and saw that she was not entered. I tried calling her, but I learned that the phone had been disconnected. A mutual friend, Charles Fugita, called me one day to tell me that he had moved June into his home so he could keep an eye on her. An incorrigible, extremely heavy smoker, June had, a few weeks earlier, accidentally set fire to her house. She was not injured but the fact remained that she was no longer able to take care of herself. A year or so later, through some acquaintances I had in the dog world I learned that Charles, himself quite ill, had been forced to move June into a nursing home. I tried calling her there several times but was never able to be connected. I wrote to her and received, at first, no reply. I continued to send birthday and Christmas cards and an occasional letter. Eventually, my mail was returned as "Unknown". I am still sad when I think about June and her exciting and varied life with an ending about which one has to wonder, "Is that all there was?"

EPILOGUE

ADULTHOOD—FINALLY

Don and I moved to Southern California in June of 1975 mostly for economic reasons. I hated to leave my beloved San Francisco Bay Area, a part of the world that had finally welcomed me and encouraged me through very difficult times in my life. Everything I knew and loved, not to mention most of the people who were important to me, were in the Bay Area. Starting anew again did not have much appeal for me; but that was what we had decided to do. It turned out to be a good move and one that enabled me to shake off at least a good part of the baggage from my childhood and adolescence.

Things did not go absolutely smoothly right away. A few years earlier we had made a trip to the high desert, near Palm Springs, to visit Kay Baker, an Italian Greyhound breeder I had met at a show and with whom I had become friendly over the years. Kay, a retired hospital administrator, had been living her lifelong dream of owning a boarding kennel by buying and refurbishing a rundown breeding establishment in the little town of Yucca Valley. Don and I had loaded our dogs into the motorhome and had driven south. We camped in nearby Joshua Tree National Monument (now a National Park) and had a wonderful vacation along with visiting Kay and talking dogs a good part of the time. Kay was very persuasive in telling us we should invest in desert property for eventual retirement. This was, even in the 1970's, a still affordable part of California. On our way out of town we had stopped at a real estate office on the highway and had wound up making an offer on a secluded five acre hilltop in Morongo Valley, a piece of property that had a fabulous view of Mt. San Jacinto, the often snow-covered mountain that overlooks Palm Springs and the Coachella Valley. Much to our surprise, our apparently lowball offer had been accepted, and we had become owners of the sandy, scrub-covered land that was reachable only by a spiderweb network of dirt roads and trails.

Within a year we had gotten the bright idea of having a shell house built on our hilltop, which was to become a giant do-it-yourself kit that we planned to finish ourselves during vacations and on long weekends. With retirement still quite a few years away, we had felt we could complete the interior of the small house by the time we would be ready to occupy it. We had had the builders complete the plumbing and wiring so it would be legal for us to move in and live there while we were finishing the flooring, drywall, ceilings and cabinetry. We could take our time with painting, wallpaper and other final décor items. It was a very appealing idea. However, at the time we decided to move to Morongo Valley permanently we had spent only one vacation and two weekends working on the house. It was not at all close to being ready for occupancy.

The sale of our home in Orinda hinged on our being able to completely vacate the premises within thirty days, including whatever cleanup was required and removal of all trash. We thought we could do it, but we had not realized how much "stuff" one can accumulate in seven or eight years of living in a place; and it took much longer to load the U-Haul than we had anticipated. We had planned to finish loading by five or six in the evening, take a short nap in the cabover camper that was installed on our Datsun pickup, and then make the 500+ mile drive to Morongo Valley during the cooler hours of the night, since neither the U-Haul truck nor the Datsun was equipped with air conditioning. Desert driving during the heat of the day can be a killer. We already knew that. However, by 9PM we weren't even close to being finished with loading in spite of our careful planning and pre-packing of nearly everything but last minute items. We decided that the comfort of our eight Italian Greyhounds was of the utmost importance and that I should put them aboard the camper and start off with Don to follow in the U-Haul as soon as he had finished loading it even if that meant his leaving several hours later or possibly the next morning. At least I would be able to get the dogs and myself through the desert during the night.

    Driving alone and the knowledge that I *have* to be somewhere by a certain time generally acts for me like a sedative; and one thing I had learned over the years was not to try to drive when I feel sleepy. Consequently, I lost several valuable hours of cool nighttime driving by stopping at various rest areas along the way to take a nap. This prompted my decision to take the somewhat longer but slightly cooler route through the Los Angeles area. That turned out to be a mistake.

    The first indication that this would be a somewhat less than smooth trip came when I decided to make a "doggie stop" at the rest area near Bakersfield at six or seven in the morning. We had carefully packed two exercise pens in the camper, the rest of our dog gear going more easily into the big moving truck. That included our entire supply of clips, which are needed to hold the exercise pens together when in use. Annoyed by the oversight, I carefully put the ends of the pens together, overlapping them and hoping to fool the dogs into thinking they were locked. It is not easy to fool an Italian Greyhound about something like that and considerably *less* easy to fool eight of them. The result was some amused onlookers and a very NON-amusing and not too merry chase around the pet area. The thought briefly entered my mind that it would have paid off to have ALL of the dogs at least partially obedience trained instead of just two of them. It was certainly too late for that.

    During the roundup a brief spat started in the other pen, crowded as it was. One of the girls, Nova, who had until then never argued back, was hassling Candy; and someone was bleeding. It had never happened before, and I still think that Candy must have scratched her head on one of Nova's nails; but the incident was enough to add to my growing uneasiness. Something told me to crate all of them and not even to allow Speedy, my constant front seat companion, to ride loose for the remainder of the trip.

    There were no further problems, other than a broken radio antenna, and I was happy that I was making such good time when I rolled into the home stretch of Interstate 10 as it approaches the 29 Palms Highway. I wondered how late a start Don might have gotten and which route he had taken. Maybe I would still be able to make it to our new home before he got there. I had the key.

If the radio had been working, I might not have been quite so complacent; or, better yet, I would have taken the alternate route and would have avoided what followed. In the meantime, I could not believe what good time I was logging. There must have been a very good tailwind, since the speedometer was reading close to seventy and I barely had my foot on the gas. On an ordinary flat stretch of highway a Datsun pickup with a fully loaded cabover camper could barely reach the speed limit, which was 55 miles per hour for campers and trailers.

At the junction with State Highway 62, ordinarily fifteen minutes from Morongo Valley, I noticed two highway patrol cars and several other vehicles parked at the side of the road. When one of the patrolmen flagged me down, my first thought was that they finally had nailed me for going over 55. I soon wished it had been that simple. Rolling down the window, I noticed that there was a little bit more activity than a strong tailwind. In fact, the wind had a velocity I could not recall ever having experienced before. The officer was having an extremely difficult time standing upright in it, and he was no midget. He informed me that Route 62 was closed to campers and trailers, that they had lost a couple already that morning and that I had better take the alternate route although it had an overpass that would be a challenge in the wind for a tall, poorly balanced vehicle like mine. Not being familiar with the other road, I asked him if it would be all right for me to wait there for a little while until the wind subsided. He nodded and told me where and how to park.

The wind had increased, and I found it difficult even to just come to a stop. After shutting off the engine, I felt the camper rock and sway like a car at the top of a Ferris wheel. My intention was to get out of the cab and into the back of the camper to check on the dogs, but I found that I could not walk without hanging on to the side of the camper for dear life, which made me wonder whether I could even get the back door open against the wind. While I was thinking about it, the storm seemed to let up a bit and the two highway patrol cars pulled out, heading down what the officer had indicated as the alternate route. I decided to try it in spite of the dangerous overpass about which the patrolman had warned me.

Being new to the desert, I did not understand the sign I saw as I approached the Indian Avenue overpass. It said "Severe Dust Storm Area". With a two-handed death grip on the steering wheel, I inched the camper across only to find that the wind on the other side was even stronger. Not only that, but it was accompanied by billows of blowing sand and dust that made the air all around appear to consist of a solid brown fog. Cars were pulling into the gas station ahead in droves and stopping in their tracks. I thought maybe I should do likewise, so I followed suit, carefully pointing the nose of the Datsun away from the wind as the highway patrolman had told me previously I should do.

If I had thought the camper was rocking before, it now had reached motion sickness proportions. I decided I had better reassure the dogs. However, when I opened the door to get out, the wind nearly blew it off, springing the hinges and denting the front fender. It was with great difficulty that I managed to get it shut again and decided at that point that it would be foolhardy to try to open the back. If the wind was strong enough to damage the truck, the much flimsier camper door could be blown off completely, which would have made matters much worse. I thanked my lucky stars that the camper windows were partially open and that all the dogs were in sturdy crates.

Several dozen people had accumulated in the station office and most were lined up to use the pay phone. Many appeared frightened. I just wondered how long we would have to wait there. I had no thought of making a telephone call, since we did not as yet have a phone in our new home.

I am still unable to believe what happened during the next few hours. The station manager decided to close up, first transporting most of the people across the highway to another gas station. Some refused to go, afraid to leave their stranded vehicles unattended. Of course I would not leave my camper full of dogs either. About a dozen of us, including a nearly frantic Mexican woman with three small children and a sick baby, huddled into the ladies' room, which the manager had failed to lock. The woman's husband had stayed in their car; but since the blowing sand made it impossible to leave the windows open and the heat with closed windows was unbearable, the rest of the family had gone into the open restroom. The woman asked me if I thought the police would come and rescue us, and I told her that I didn't think anyone knew that there were people stranded there. At length I decided to try to get across the highway to the other station to attempt to call Kay Baker, the only person I knew that lived anywhere nearby, and to see if she could find out if Don had gotten through the storm with the U-Haul. My new Mexican friend asked if I could call the highway patrol and tell them about her sick baby.

Walking backwards to avoid getting the driving sand into my eyes and face, I arrived at the other station only to find about thirty people in line to use the single phone. I did get through to make a call to the police, but I decided not to take extra time to call Kay while people were waiting in line. By the time I got back, there was a police car on the scene to pick up the Mexican family and take them across the way to a Stuckey's store where more stormbound people were congregated. No one seemed to have any idea how long it was likely to last; but the officers said no campers, trailers or small cars should attempt to move out of the area until further notice. Several of the men were laying bets as to what would blow over first—the gas station's tall sign or the little green Datsun with the cabover camper. It really WAS swaying badly in the gale force wind, and I was beginning to become a little frantic myself. I wondered how I could manage to get four crates out of it—and where could I take them if I did? It had been about ten hours since the dogs had been out or had any water. I tried to get one of the men to help, but he was reluctant. He told me that I would not be much help to the dogs if I were inside the camper when it overturned. In their metal crates the dogs had a far better chance of being unhurt in case that were to happen; so I gave up on the idea.

Just before dark, the station sign came crashing down—fortunately missing all the remaining people and most of the parked cars. In small groups, the fugitives had started to make their way over to Stuckey's; and I decided to try it myself, if only to have access to a phone.

The scene at Stuckey's brought all the pictures I had ever seen of disaster areas meaningfully home. People were milling about aimlessly. A few had settled down under the display tables and in the aisles, bedding down on coats, a few blankets and anything else they could find. The manager was wild-eyed and seemed very much worried. He wanted to close the store—it was seven o'clock and normal closing time; but he could not throw these people out into the storm. A few teenagers were busily trying to steal merchandise, however under the surveillance of an off-duty policewoman from Indio, also stranded by the storm. She told me later that all she could do was warn the youngsters. After all—what was she to do with them if she were to arrest them? By this time quite a number of people were aware of my concern over the dogs in the camper and most of them shared my worry. It was dark outside by then, and I could no longer see the unsteady and constantly rocking camper. When an occasional newcomer arrived, I questioned him as to whether there were any overturned vehicles on the Union station lot. No one had seen any.

At 11PM, with the winds not in the least abated, two buses arrived, one of the drivers announcing that everyone would be taken to Beaumont, 25 miles away, to be guests of the Red Cross and the City of Beaumont for the night. Stuckey's was closing, and anyone not going would have no alternative but to stay out in the storm. I decided to take my chances in the camper until a woman suggested that I ask the driver if I could take the dogs—that her husband would help me get them out of the camper. I asked, and the reply was, "I don't see why not". He drove the bus over to where the Datsun was parked, still upright, fortunately; and I asked for three more volunteers. Three teen aged boys came along, and with two of them holding the door, we got the crates out and into the bus. There was about a three-inch depth of sand all over everything inside the camper, including in the bottom of the crates. The dogs were, surprisingly, rather unperturbed.

We spent the night in an old schoolhouse in Beaumont, on cots supplied by the Red Cross. I had plenty of help carrying the crates in, and we shared an area indicated for dogs with two German Shepherds and their owners. Just about every youngster in the place (there were about 70 people in all) volunteered to help me with the dogs. They were badly in need of being walked. Fortunately, I had a leash in my pocket; so, with six children and a nice woman who said she was a cocker spaniel breeder to hold the other seven IGs, I walked the gang one at a time, all of them completely cooperative.

Several of the kids brought water in paper cups, but there was no sign of food until around 2AM, when the sandwiches arrived. By that time, I had passed out on my cot and by the time I woke up in the morning, all that was left was peanut butter and jelly. I didn't think my Italian Greyhounds would be particular by then; but I had some doubts as to what the volunteer workers would think about my feeding sandwiches to the dogs. So, I surreptitiously stuffed my pockets with sandwiches and passed them out to the gang in their crates. Even the three month old puppy seemed to enjoy this change of fare.

For the next few hours we kept having various announcements as to wind and weather conditions, with promises that the buses would take us back to our cars as soon as we would be able to drive them out. Of course, there were warnings about driving cars that had been in a sandstorm—and further warning that all the nearby garages and service stations would be busy for days doing the necessary cleanup job on local vehicles that had been left outdoors. The cocker woman and I walked down the block to buy dog food as soon as we felt that stores would be open; and at last I was able to get a call through to Kay. She promised to drive to Morongo to see if Don had got there yet and to tell him what had happened to me.

Until about two in the afternoon I spent my time walking dogs, supervising the army of children wanting to play with them, and doing a bit of worrying about the Datsun.

A television news crew arrived and filmed the scene, including an interview with the now rather decrepit looking woman with the eight little dogs, none of which seemed any the worse for wear. Quite a few people, I think, became Italian Greyhound fans in those hours, marveling at how quiet the dogs were through all of this and how little mess they had made. Shortly after two in the afternoon, a friend of the cocker breeder arrived to take her home and, since she had a big station wagon, she offered to take me and my dogs along or to drop us off at our own house.

Other than the fact that wires got crossed and Don and Kay were on their way to Beaumont to pick us up at the same time as we were on our way home in the station wagon, that was the end of the adventure. The camper was incapacitated for another few days, when we finally were able to have it towed to nearby Palm Springs to be cleaned out enough to be driven. Insurance paid for the mechanical cleanup and the extensive paint and body damage; but it would be years before sand stopped leaking from every conceivable nook, cranny or crevice every time the Datsun and camper were used.

∽⦅⦆∾

In a way our move to Southern California was, for me, the start of yet another new life. Originally it was not a change that was made from free choice, and I was very sad to have to leave the Bay Area, which I had grown to love as the first place I had ever lived where I could feel safe and reasonably secure; but this time when change was needed I had experienced situations and people who had given me the background with which to be able to face a new beginning and its challenges. My years with Carter's and with Technicolor had taught me a great deal about the ins and outs of the working world; and the people in my life during that time— although I have not introduced all of them in these pages—had given me a much more positive grasp on the art of successful relationships.

Among the people about whom I should have written are the late Maestro Arturo Casiglia, director of the Pacific Opera Company, and Bay Area soprano Dorothy Warenskjold, who was well known to opera buffs of the 1940's and 50's not only as a star of the San Francisco Opera Company but from numerous radio and television appearances as well. Maestro Casiglia was one of the first to recognize my abilities not only with a camera but with words; and he soon had me doing publicity for his shoestring opera company, which, in turn, led to my job with Opera & Concert Magazine. My friendship with Dorothy Warenskjold is ongoing, mostly in the form of e-mail, since she has retired away from California. One of my fondest recollections of this consummate artist and truly wonderful person involves an unauthorized trip I made on a work day, after calling in sick, to attend a recital she was giving in Red Bluff, about 200 miles north of San Francisco. After a fabulous musical evening and a few minutes at the reception local music fans gave for Dorothy, I headed for home in my nearly new British Ford only to drop the transmission and subsequently the entire car and myself into a ditch alongside the highway out of town. I was very young, had very little money and knew absolutely no one in Red Bluff. After having the car towed to a local Ford dealership at nearly midnight, I had no idea where to go or what to do next. I decided to head for the lobby of the hotel where I knew

Dorothy was staying. I had no intention of contacting her, but it was at least somewhere to go and, hopefully, no one would hassle me. I sat on one of the sofas that was furthest from the registration desk and tried, rather vainly, to relax while studying the concert program from that evening.

Dorothy, her accompanist and her manager returned from the reception about half an hour after I had arrived at the hotel. She saw me immediately and quickly made her way over to where I was sitting.

"I thought you were going home," she said pleasantly. Her look indicated that she had a feeling that I was not there by choice.

I felt my face turning several shades of red. "My car broke down just south of town," I told her. "I'm sort of stuck here."

She asked me if I had a room and I was forced to admit that I didn't have the money for one. This was still in the pre-credit card era.

Dorothy sat down next to me. She told her manager, also named Dorothy, to check at the desk to see if she could get me a room near theirs. We spent another hour talking, during which Dorothy said she would check in the morning about getting another plane ticket so I could fly back to San Francisco with them. The flight was late enough in the morning that I would have a chance to find out about my car first. We all knew that it was very likely that the car could not be repaired for several days, especially since it was still under warranty and Red Bluff did not have a British Ford dealership. We had a leisurely breakfast in the morning and confirmed with the local Ford dealer that it would be some time during the following week before the car could be ready. Parts would have to be ordered from San Francisco. Normally I would have worried myself sick over the situation, but Dorothy's friendly confidence and positive attitude managed to turn the episode into almost a fun recollection rather than the disaster it might have been.

I had also learned to cope with negativity and adversity when they occurred and could not be avoided. My involvement in the dog world continued to grow. Using what I had learned I became a successful participant in the dog sport, first as a breeder and exhibitor and then as a writer, an officer in several dog clubs and even a judge. Thanks to the pursuit of my devotion to Italian Greyhounds I was invited to travel to England, Italy, Australia and

Brazil. In addition to the dog involvement I was even able to follow my lifelong love of animals in general by making several trips to Africa and participating in some photo safaris, something I had longed to do since childhood and had always felt would never be possible for someone like myself. For a year I held the dream job of feature writer for a newspaper, the Hi Desert Star in Yucca Valley—a position that ended when it was discovered that I did not possess a degree in journalism, an issue I had managed to avoid when interviewing for the job. Thanks to Jean Buttz, a good friend of mine who was head of the English language department at Thomas Jefferson Middle School in Decatur, Illinois until she retired a few years ago, I had the opportunity for several years to do an annual presentation on the Holocaust for all of the 8th grade students as well as some younger children in Decatur while they were studying world events of the first half of the Twentieth Century. This gave me a chance to try my hand at teaching. I had once felt I would like to be a teacher but had given up the idea when it became doubtful that I would be able to obtain a college education.

During the process of preparing to give the Holocaust talk and subsequent question and answer sessions I think I gained more knowledge of that dark part of history and about its effect on my family and on me than I had ever realized. Each time I did the program was an emotional catharsis, especially when it was brought home to me that I was making a lasting impression on my young, mostly inner city audience, many of whom had until then felt that they were the only ones in the world affected by prejudice and bigotry. My interaction with people in most situations became easier and more rewarding, and I was finally able to see some of the world as a participant rather than as an outsider standing on my tiptoes in order to watch from the windows without being seen. It has taken a while, but I think I've finally grown up.

These days I spend a great deal of time with my Italian Greyhounds— showing them, writing about them and just loving them.

ISBN 1412099997-8